The Tragedy of Janie Sharp

The Mystery Continues: Murder in Rural Hill

By

W.W. McCully

Cover by W. W. McCully

Published by W. W. McCully

www.wwmccully.com

ISBN:

979-8-3916937-1-0

979-8-9871010-3-2

979-8-9871010-2-5

TABLE OF CONTENTS

Dedicated to my wife, Tracy and my daughter, Myrrah who just let the ol' man do his thing.

A special thank you to Penny Sharp

PREFACE

When a true crime event remains unsolved for more than one hundred years, that mystery becomes folklore. Facts become muddled and speculation is often accepted as truth. When far removed from the actual event, the telling of the tale with embellishment takes on a life of its own, overshadowing the tragic end of the victim(s), the effect on the remaining families and community and the perpetrator(s) who escaped justice.

During my research both before and after the publication of the book, "Murder in Rural Hill," I was contacted by a significant number of people who believed that they had specific information relative to the case; information that was almost always unknown to others.

This was rarely the case. Some claimed to have documents that never materialized. Some provided material that was already in my possession. Others shared bits and pieces of information passed from one generation of their family to the next that may or may not have been pertinent to the case but all without supporting documentation.

Many were convinced of Swinton Permenter's guilt while others were just as adamant about his innocence and the involvement of other parties.

After the publication in 2016, there were however, some slivers of additional information that surfaced, providing support to already accepted assumptions and conclusion while some conflicted directly with "known facts" of the case. All adding intrigue and a deepening of the mystery of Janie Sharp's death.

I am thankful for the interest and the passion of those who sought to add their memories and family lore to the story of a century old murder case.

Not long after the publication of "Murder in Rural Hill," I was approached by Penny Sharp. Penny was not a member of the Sharp family but a descendent of Walton Permenter, who was a victim in this affair – brutally murdered in 1912.

Her openness and graciousness resulted in much of the new material included in this book; photographs and documents that had not seen the light of day for more than a hundred years.

She provided insight into the effects that the trial and the death of Walton Permenter had on her family throughout the years. I am grateful for her time and assistance.

I have received some criticism for the complexity of the tale presented in the previous book. I believe some expected the work to read like a novel, a work of fiction, but Murder in Rural Hill was a presentation of an actual event – a life event that will always be complex, messy, and subject to debate. The conflicting information and detailed testimony, the bevy of names and relationships are all factual and part of the story.

"The Tragedy of Janie Sharp" is an attempt to incorporate new information, images and background. You will find that much of the text is unchanged but you will also find additional local history, images and correspondence, information relative to a possible eyewitness and more insight into the aftermath of the murders and trials of 1910-1912.

"Sleep On, Dear Janie, Thy Work is Done

Thy Mortal Pangs are O'er

Jesus Has Come And Borne Thee Home

Beyond This World Of Sin And Woe"

INTRODUCTION

When one visits the rural communities of western Winston County, Mississippi, it is not hard to imagine that you have traveled a hundred years into the past. Of course, there are modern homes, much of the farmland has been planted in pine timber and satellite dishes sprout from the yards and rooftops. Today, many roads are paved but the area is not heavily populated and families still tend to cluster together. The wooded land, small fields, swamps and the tree-shrouded narrow roads dominate the landscape much as they did at the beginning of the 20th century.

But find a quiet spot and step away from all the noise and distractions of modern life and it becomes easy to imagine a distant time – a farmer in the field across the way, giving a coarse gee-haw to a stubborn gray mule pulling a plow, the squealing and shouting of young boys enjoying an afternoon swim in Lobutcha Creek or a young girl with her parasol taking an afternoon stroll to the nearest country store.

No time in history was truly innocent. Yet in the early 1900's, at that time and at that place, daily life was much simpler and generally free of the fears and complications that define modern existence.

The comfortable simplicity of that time was shattered on a hot July day in 1910.

Rural communities tend to mark time and be defined by major events in their history. Most of them horrific - battles, feuds, fires, murders and natural disasters. The nearby community of Louisville will be marked for years to come by a tornado in 2014 that destroyed hundreds of homes, took a dozen lives and destroyed industry and medical services. It changed that community forever – yielding good and bad.

The tiny settlement of Rural Hill would eventually fade away like most such places. All that remains is a small brick church that no longer holds regular services. However, the community remains in spirit. Homes are scattered across the surrounding countryside, the last vestiges of working farms and family land. The community that remains is forever defined by one event – the brutal murder of a young woman.

***

My interest in the death of Janie Sharp was initially limited – just another ghost tale that folks like to repeat. But in 2010, Center Ridge United Methodist Church, where Janie was laid to rest so many years ago, held an acknowledgement of the 100th anniversary of her death.

At the church that day, a number of people spoke and related the anecdotal tales passed down within their families, sometimes with conflicting "facts." A niece of Janie's was in attendance but had little to add to the tale as her family seldom spoke of the trauma.

I quickly realized that no real effort had been made to record the true story of Janie. Compilations of newspaper clippings and repeated tales had been published but the chronology of events, an understanding of the times, the people involved and the effect her death and subsequent events had on the community were not documented.

It was a horrific event that took the life of a vibrant young woman, ultimately led to the murder of at least two other individuals and destroyed the lives of several more including a young man accused of the act.

This is a story that some did not want told and for many years, open public discussion was discouraged. The families involved maintained deep ties and roots in the area. Feelings were strong and the unresolved nature of the case led to speculation and speculation led to conflict between kin and even between husbands and wives.

In my research, at least one party spoke of his grandparents, people who toiled and worked the land together, raised children, served their church and their community, people who had few cross words in their marriage except about the guilt or innocence of a young man accused of a long-ago murder.

Until the late 1970's, students at the local schools were forbidden to write essays or promote discussion about the case by the district superintendent for fear of opening old wounds.

The conflict, the imposed censorship and the unresolved mystery had the opposite effect and kept the story of Janie Sharp alive. It was passed across kitchen tables and across quilt stands at sewing parties. It surfaced on front porches on Sunday afternoons, underneath shade trees, around feed store counters, country store gas pumps, hunting camps or anywhere that old men gathered.

The stories and legends continue today.

My motivation to do further research peaked not at that church meeting but on a crisp evening in October.

Without a doubt, October is the finest month of the year in central Mississippi. The almost religious fervor for high school and SEC football coincides with warm, dry days and crisp cool nights when the first campfires of the season dispel the chill of autumn's approach.

It was Halloween. The week had been filled with hayrides, carnivals, silly or macabre costumes and children energized by a sugar overload. It was a time of fun but it was also a time of dread for those in positions of responsibility for Center Ridge Methodist Church.

Directly across a dusty, rural, gravel road lay the remains of Perninah Jane (Janie) Sharp. Her tombstone is easily identifiable, a tall marble obelisk located by the roadside behind a chain link fence that surrounds several acres of near ancient markers inscribed with familiar family names.

Over the years, to visit the grave of Janie Sharp has become a rite of passage for many high school students in the county. Ghost stories were rampant and the most prominent was that Janie would rise from the grave on Halloween night and search for her killer.

While church members didn't mind the stories or the teenage visitors, the litter, beer cans and vandalism were another matter. In an effort to curtail these problems, church members held their own event, passing out candy to the little ones and gathering around a bonfire in the church yard in hopes of modifying the behavior of those who came to exhibit their bravery in confrontation with the ghost of a long dead teenage girl.

Sitting around that bonfire, I watched as wave after wave of kids and adults arrived by the carload in hopes of catching a glimpse of Janie; something – anything to make their heart pound, to get that adrenalin rush, to tell their friends about in school on Monday. Cell phones flashed to capture images of a tombstone but more often than not – to capture images of themselves on a great adventure.

As I watched I also listened to the conflicting tales told around that fire:

She was found in her wedding dress.

No – she was carrying her wedding dress because she was on her way to have it altered.

She was found hanging in a tree, a noose around her neck.

No – she was hanging in a tree alright - not by a noose but by her long blonde hair.

She was killed by a spurned lover.

It became apparent that the real story, the most interesting story, was lost in the legends. As the years unfolded, the story grew bigger, more fantastic and convoluted until it became little more than a cautionary ghost tale to frighten children and make hearts race around a late evening campfire.

Over the years, the facts had become unclear, encased in legend and subject to the desire to make a good story even more fantastic. This book is an attempt to tell the story of Janie and the aftermath of her murder in as straightforward a manner as possible.

In my research, I believe I discovered several things:

There were some underlying circumstances that never made it to the surface. I won't speculate on those and the reader can form their own opinions.

The newspapers of the day tended to sensationalize the story and some reported information was inaccurate, based upon trial testimony.

The community was divided into two camps and both held their beliefs strongly.

The nature of the conflicting testimony indicates that at least some parties lied under oath, whether in an attempt to hide their own involvement or to guarantee the conviction of a party that they honestly believed was guilty is not discernable.

"Because of" or "in spite of" the final trial verdict, the legal system in Mississippi at that time worked in the manner in which it was intended. The judges, prosecution and defense lawyers performed admirably in almost all situations.

Pending the discovery of some long lost (and long rumored) written confession, we will never know for certain who killed Janie Sharp.

I have tried to present the facts as clearly as possible. Whenever there was conflicting information or testimony, I attempted to indicate this. Some issues have never been raised or examined closely and I will attempt to do so in this narrative. It should also be remembered that **there was not one unsolved murder but three: Janie Sharp, Walton Permenter and Ben Walker.**

Speculation as to who the guilty party or parties might be in these cases has been a popular pastime throughout the years – even today. Names have surfaced, tales of anonymous confessions, rumors of a deathbed confession and repetition of second and third hand reports from grandparents and long deceased family members keep the mystery and debate alive and well. This is likely how it should remain. Private surmises and family legends as to guilt or innocence should remain just that – private.

The murder of a young Janie Sharp and the ensuing trials and murders made national headlines, split a community for the better part of the 20th century and produced one of the most celebrated court cases in Mississippi history. Publicly, her murder and those of the others remain unresolved to this day.

CHAPTER 1.
Rural Hill and Winston County

From a modern-day perspective, the summer of 1910 seemed an innocent time. Life was slow and quiet in the rural South, full of long sleepy days between the rush of spring planting and fall harvest. The Civil War was a distant memory and World War One was not yet on the horizon.

At first observation, the year brought many changes that did not seem to have any significant impact on a sleepy, pastoral community tucked away in the hills, hollows and swamps of central Mississippi.

The century was still young, but American life – even life in Rural Hill, Mississippi was changing much faster than most could imagine. The country was just beginning to embrace the 20th Century – a time that would yield great industry, technology and social and political turmoil.

The railroad had come to the county seat of Louisville just five years earlier. The rail line was late coming to Winston County. As the massive forests of south Mississippi were dwindling, access to the timberlands of central areas of the state was needed. Rail brought easier travel and entry to markets that were not available prior to 1905, spurring growth in the area.

While aviation was in its infancy, 1910 seemed to bring new firsts every month; fastest flight, greatest height, crossing of the English Channel, first passenger flight, first seaplane, first night flight, first takeoff from a sea going vessel and as harbingers of things to come, the first patent for a machine gun placement in an aircraft and the first bombs dropped in flight.

The month of April saw the death of America's first true literary icon, Samuel Langhorne Clemens and the return of Halley's Comet after a 75-year absence. Clemens (Mark Twain) was born shortly after the comet's appearance in 1835 and died only a day after it reached its closest proximity to Earth in 1910. The year before his death, Twain was quoted: *"I came in with Halley's Comet in 1835. It is coming again next year, and I expect to go out with it. It will be the greatest disappointment of my life if I don't go out with Halley's Comet. The Almighty has said, no doubt: "Now here are these two unaccountable freaks; they came in together, they must go out together."*

Politically and socially, the nation was changing as well. President William Howard Taft's conservative leanings were beginning to form a rift in the Republican Party that eventually led to the formation of the Bull Moose Party. The split of Republican votes would ultimately guarantee Democrat Woodrow Wilson's election in 1912.

Baseball was king and Cy Young was the crown prince as he recorded his 500th win on July 19th. Just two weeks before that – the social order of the country was challenged when a black man, Jack Johnson defeated the white Heavyweight Champ James J. Jeffries with a knockout in the 15th round. Deemed the fight of the century and held before a crowd of 20,000 in Reno, Nevada, Johnson became the undisputed Heavyweight Champion.

There was civil unrest as well. October would bring what many regarded as the first case of domestic terrorism in the country as a bomb ripped through the offices of the Los Angeles Times. Placed by union sympathizers, the blast and resulting fire killed twenty-one employees.

All these things were very distant to the farmers, sharecroppers and storekeepers in the tiny communities spread across Mississippi and the South. These bits and pieces of interest arrived once or twice a week in newspapers from such exotic places as Memphis or Jackson. They may have generated an occasional comment beneath the glow of a coal oil lamp or on a front porch on a Sunday afternoon but were little more than distractions to folks who lived and struggled to succeed upon the land. Few could envision how a flying contraption or a sporting event could have any significant impact on their lives.

But change was taking place, even across the most rural parts of the South. A few folks had telephones in their homes although most had to travel to the community store to make or take a phone call. There were some "horseless carriages" but the mule was still the most useful tool on the farm.

In the rolling hills of east Mississippi, farm size was limited by a family's ability to work it, so the volume of land under cultivation was generally small even for those with broods of children or the benefits of tenant farmers and sharecroppers. Cotton was the cash crop while corn and sorghum were grown for livestock and human consumption.

The Rural Hill Community in western Winston County was not much different than the hundreds of others scattered across the state and the county.

In many ways, Rural Hill was indistinguishable from Mill Creek, Coopwood, Hinze, Marydell, Liberty, Fearn Springs and the forty odd others that dotted the county located in east central Mississippi – these communities strategically located every few miles based upon distance and the flow and flood patterns of any number of creeks and minor rivers.

Situated not far from the historic Natchez Trace and the Robinson Road that connected the growing town of Columbus and points east with Jackson, Mississippi, the Rural Hill area continued to be sparsely populated until the late 1800's.

The Trace began as a buffalo trail, first used by the multitude of Native American tribes (predominantly Choctaw and Chickasaw) of the area and then as a route in the late 1700's and early 1800's for returning raft men taking that long walk back to Nashville and points beyond after floating their goods downriver to the settlement of Natchez.

Sometimes known as "The Devil's Backbone," tales from the heyday of the Trace - of buried treasure, highwaymen such as the infamous Harp brothers and Samuel Mason were certainly common in the early days of the settlement. The famous outlaw, John Murrell was reported to have ventured from the Trace on occasion and was even reported to have kept a secret hideout in the Smallwood area of southwest Winston County not far from Rural Hill.

Smallwood was named after a man who kept a stand along the Robinson Road in the early 1800's. Rumors of his buried gold surfaced after he became deranged and was killed by Choctaw authorities sent to arrest him. Numerous attempts to find the fortune were fruitless over the years.

In latter days, stories of captured Yankee gold and tales of midnight visits of the James gang and their possible family connections in the area were told in hushed tones.

A post office, two general stores, a spoke factory, a two-room schoolhouse and the Rural Hill Methodist Church were central to the small farms raising cotton for sale, corn and hay for livestock and vegetables for personal consumption. Land in the area was first purchased in 1838 and more settlers came to the area in 1860. These included the Blaine, Lowery, Williams and Ray families.

The makeup of Rural Hill served the community well on a daily basis until the need or desire overtook folk and a visit to the more populated towns of Louisville or Kosciusko was required.

Louisville was the county seat of Winston County and boasted a growing population of 1181 in 1910. Situated fourteen miles east of Rural Hill, Louisville had its beginnings as early as 1828 when the entire area was still Indian territory. After the Treaty of Dancing Rabbit in 1830 and the resettlement of most of the Choctaw Indians from the area, the land was officially opened to white settlers. A few whites had settled in the area prior to the treaty and taken Choctaw women as wives.

After the treaty, the flood gates were opened and families, adventurers and fortune seekers from eastern states such as South Carolina, Virginia and Georgia came to central Mississippi in hopes of finding cheap fertile land and new opportunities. My own ancestors came to the area in 1832 and the early 1840's searching for land and opportunities that could no longer be found along the country's eastern seaboard. With a growing population, Louisville was incorporated in 1836.

During its early years, like all frontier towns, Louisville was far from a civilized, genteel antebellum community as southern society is so often portrayed. Fights on the streets, usually of the fisticuff nature, were a common occurrence at any time of the day. Alcohol, the usual precursor of these fights, was available at any number of saloons scattered around town, in taverns or the back corner of stores. Whiskey could be bought for ten cents a drink or fifty cents per gallon. Prior to the Civil War, a forty-gallon whiskey barrel was placed in the courthouse yard during court days and free whiskey could be expected any time a group of men gathered to trade cotton or other goods.

Compared to many other parts of the South, the area was relatively unscathed by the Civil War, except for the loss of many young men who had quickly volunteered for the Confederacy. The only significant local contact with the dreaded "Yankees" occurred in 1863 as Grierson's Raiders passed through the area in route to Baton Rouge. The raid would later become the fictionalized subject of a Hollywood movie titled "The Horse Soldiers" starring John Wayne and William Holden.

Although the Union cavalry moved quickly through the county, working their way from northeast to southwest, many homesteaders were subjected to confiscation of property as small bands of Union troops scavenged for food and horses.

Some were forewarned of the oncoming Yankees and there remain many tales of hiding livestock in the woods and hollows and burying silverware, hams and other food stock before they arrived. Even my own great-great grandfather suffered at the hands of marauders as four or five soldiers removed all the long guns and pistols from the house and broke them against the trunk of a mulberry tree in the yard.

Despite Colonel Grierson's frantic ride through Mississippi in the Spring of 1863, Winston County suffered little in comparison to the cities of Jackson, Meridian and Vicksburg or the states of Georgia and South Carolina when Sherman cut a wide swath through the countryside.

The immediate years following the war were difficult for blacks and whites alike. Farms, roads and bridges had been neglected through the war years and the loss of so many young men and the loss of slave labor slowed the process of rebuilding.

The freed slaves tended to fall into three categories; many returned to the farms of their previous owners and worked for wages or as sharecroppers - building their own communities and farms over time. Some left the area looking for a better life elsewhere and some attempted to survive on the hope and false promises of the carpetbaggers and scalawags of Reconstruction.

By the local elections of 1875, whites seeking to regain control and blacks who had finally had their fill of the false promises of the Republicans voted to return power back to the Democrats. Without question, the actions of the Klu Klux Klan had some impact on these elections as well.

The early Klan (first appearing in Winston County around 1870) was generally non-violent but as the years passed their activities became more vicious and senseless. Through the Federal Enforcement Acts and the citizens' general disgust with the Klan's activities, the KKK's presence began to wane across the area by the 1880's.

Unfortunately, in Winston County, some groups formed and continued to use acts of intimidation against the black community. One local group known as "The Iron Band Gang" degenerated into threats and acts of violence not only against the black population but also against poor whites.

There is very little that is known today about the Iron Band. The consensus of opinion is that their tactics were employed as a land grab. Initially these tactics were only aimed at blacks, whipping them and running them off their property.

Over time, they became even more brazen. Poor whites would be visited in the dead of night. Their livestock might be killed, fences destroyed and barns and outbuildings fired. In fear for their lives, victims would sell their property at rock bottom prices – always to members or friends of the gang.

The matter came to a head in 1899 resulting in a series of bloody murders that became known as the Johnson - Wicker Feud. Newspaper reports were limited and vague, likely due to fear of retribution but did indicate that the more "law abiding" elements of the community formed a secret society of their own with the intent of ridding the community of the Iron Band Gang. Members of the gang were ambushed on the roads and in the fields as they worked. This ultimately brought the Iron Band to its knees.

No local citizens were ever convicted in the matter and the general opinion was that a service had been rendered to the community and any conviction would be highly unlikely in any case.

In general, however, by the 1900's, Louisville and Winston County citizens lived a quiet existence – working the land, felling timber and raising large families. Disputes were limited in nature and were usually handled within the community. For most, church was the center of their lives – providing social and spiritual structure.

However, in 1908, a love triangle resulting in three deaths in the same family made local headlines. In the Noxubee Hills area of Winston County (north of Louisville), two young men sought the affections of a local young lady. The matter was complicated by the fact that the men were first cousins. The sought-after young woman, Betty Taylor, ultimately chose one of the cousins, Meredith Whitten.

The wedding took place, followed by a party at the home of her father, Tobe Taylor. In attendance were family members including the jilted cousin, Johnny Whitten and his two brothers, Ed and Bose. As was usually the case, the presence of alcohol led to problems and Johnny and his brothers were ordered to leave the party.

Later that evening, after the party, Meredith and his new bride along with his father, Jack Whitten, were returning to the family home when they encountered the three brothers along the way. Reports indicated that Jack jumped from the wagon and walked toward the brothers in hopes of calming the situation. As he approached, Bose shot him in the stomach. As Jack fell, he pulled a pistol and shot Bose. Meredith jumped from the wagon and the brothers, Johnny and Ed both fired upon him, killing him instantly. Jack died on the scene as well and Bose lingered for a few hours.

The remaining brothers, Johnny and Ed, fled and went into hiding for more than a year. After fifteen months they surrendered to authorities. They both served time in Parchman prison before receiving parole in 1912. In a final twist, the young widow ultimately married Meredith's brother Bill. All three victims were buried in the Noxubee Hills Cemetery in northwest Winston County.

--

By 1910, Louisville had recently experienced significant growth with the arrival of the railroad. The vast forests of giant pines and hardwoods in the southern half of the state had encouraged rail construction in the late 1800's but the railroad had managed to bypass much of the central part of Mississippi until after the turn of the century. Designated at mile marker 219.3, by 1909, Louisville was served by the New Orleans Mobile & Chicago Railroad.

Rail brought easier access to cotton markets but that benefit was limited. Winston County was not the land of rich dark soil like the Mississippi Delta to the west or the Black Prairie just to its east. Its rolling hills and swamps were not conducive to the planting of vast fields of cotton. These facts, combined with the recent and ongoing invasion of the boll weevil, limited cotton production. Folks in Winston County and Rural Hill were never able to reap the riches of white gold while sitting on the veranda of their plantation home.

For some, timber was a fine alternative. The deforestation of south Mississippi and the country's continued demand for lumber served to create a strong and steady market for the shortleaf pines that grew so well in the red clay soils of east central Mississippi.

Sawmills and the logging industry provided much needed cash for the area and created fortunes in the 20th century for a few. Better management practices, suitable topography and red soil that can produce pine trees like no other place in the country have perpetuated that industry into modern times.

But in 1910, farmers could survive and even prosper with hard work in this land. One farm family that did well in the Rural Hill community was the Sharp family.

The Will Sharp farm was located approximately a mile southwest of Rural Hill Church. The comfortable house with its long front gallery was situated on what is now known as the Edgar Steed Road and was home to William Clifton Sharp, his wife, Martha Ezell Ball Sharp, and eight surviving children in 1910. At least one child, a daughter, died in infancy.

One of those children was a popular young woman named Perninah Jane. Known to most as "Janie," she was eighteen in the summer of 1910. Like many rural and cultured young ladies, she was well-mannered and religious. She was an expert seamstress and had some musical training. According to various accounts, she was a strong, healthy girl who caught the eyes of several young men. The only known photos of Janie show a dark-haired young woman with strong features.

Later newspaper reports and conflicting court testimony indicated that she was engaged to a young man named Earl Ray from another prominent family in the area. Over the years, that report has been disputed.

Regardless, it is believed that she was well liked, well thought of by her peers and elders and had every expectation of a traditional but happy future. Those expectations ended on a hot July afternoon on a lonely country road just outside of Rural Hill, Mississippi.

Images of Perninah Jane "Janie" Sharp

CHAPTER 2.
The Murder

It was a warm Thursday afternoon (July 21) and Janie had just helped her mother, Martha, clean away the dishes from the noon meal and straighten the house. The men folk in the family had returned to the fields. July was long past planting time but the fieldwork never ended as cotton needed chopping and middles needed to be "laid by" with the plow and mule.

Following a regular habit, Janie took the opportunity to travel to the little post office and general stores in Rural Hill where she could pick up the family's mail, make a few purchases, likely socialize with whomever she met along the way and be home in time to help her mother prepare and serve the evening meal.

Rural Free Delivery (RFD) was officially established in 1896 but it was 1901 before rural delivery came to Mississippi and it was a slow process. Full rural delivery had not yet reached Rural Hill in the summer of 1910. That regular trip to the P.O. served a social purpose as well and was as much a part of life across the South as Sunday church attendance.

Taking her parasol, a few coins and a delicate handkerchief that would play a key role in the story, Janie walked the mile to Rural Hill, taking a path from her home through the woods and fields that joined Commodore Road leading northward. Her mother indicated that Janie had planned to purchase a few dress goods. There was some indication that instead of returning immediately home, she intended to stop at the home of Cyrus Ray to do some dressmaking. (In various reports, Cyrus Ray was indicated as not only an uncle to Janie but also as an uncle to her fiancée, Earl Ray.)

Little more than a narrow dirt wagon path, Commodore Road wound along a low ridge with shallow ravines branching occasionally into the surrounding woods and thickets. The path was predominantly shaded as it wound through hardwood thickets and skirted small fields and pastures. Little remains of that road today but occasional depressions along that ridge through mostly private property.

Janie was a regular customer and she drew no special attention as she conducted her business and made her purchases. She visited both stores in Rural Hill, searching for the needed sewing goods. When she left the Williams' General Store around three o'clock, she was observed by several individuals who noted that she had her parasol, two small packages of purchased items, a copy of The Weekly Commercial Appeal (a Memphis paper), two letters for the family and a handkerchief used to wrap a few coins in her possession.

According to later trial testimony, Janie told at least one individual that she intended to stop by a neighbor's home and make a phone call. The assumption was that this would likely be the Cyrus Ray home where she had told her mother she might stop. The Ray property was actually located south of the Sharp property and would require her to stay on Commodore Road well past the turnoff to her home.

She never made it to the Ray's property nor was there any indication as to why or who she may have intended to call. When Janie left that tiny village of Rural Hill in mid-afternoon on July 21, 1910, she was never seen alive again by anyone other than the person or persons who took her life.

When Janie had not returned by late afternoon, her mother grew anxious. She left her chores and walked the Commodore Road to Rural Hill in search of her. (In some reports, she first sent some of the younger children.) Not finding Janie along the way and discovering at the general store that she had indeed headed toward home, her concern grew.

By the time darkness fell that evening, the whole community knew that Janie was missing. Men started to gather from around the area and began to form search parties to scour the countryside looking for Janie.

Over the years, different reports, gossip and conflicting trial testimony began to confuse the tale at this point. The preponderance of the evidence supports the following events:

It was near dusk when the search for Janie began as groups of men gathered on and along Commodore Road. Telephone lines across the communities of Rural Hill and nearby Hinze were humming with the news of her disappearance and requests for men to join the search. A long and unproductive night lay before them.

As in all such cases, rumors began to circulate. From the early hours of the search, some believed that Janie may have disappeared of her own accord. While never explicitly stated in later trial testimony, it was obvious by their actions that some in the community believed that Janie may have eloped with someone other than her current fiancée, Earl Ray. Reliable reports indicated that Will Sharp

(Janie's father) contacted the Winston County Circuit Clerk that evening to find out if a marriage license had been issued.

This seems strange given that Earl Ray, her proclaimed fiancée, was an early member of the search party. Sharp's actions suggest that; either this call was made prior to his knowledge of Earl Ray's presence or he had suspicions that Janie had interest in another young man from the community.

Over the years, the rumor of another love interest was perpetuated by claimed conversations that Janie's engagement to Ray was a ruse. Many believed that Janie was secretly involved with another young man and that her parents did not approve of the relationship.

One of the men aiding in the search for Janie was Doctor William M. Clemmons. Clemmons, a dentist, was a long time and respected resident of Winston County and he had served at one time as the postmaster at Rural Hill.

Prior to joining the search, Dr. Clemmons made an attempt to contact the local Methodist minister named Oaks, thinking that perhaps Janie had eloped as well. He was not able to locate the minister and no indication was ever provided as to why he thought that elopement was a possibility. It is likely that Clemmons was acting upon the request of Janie's father.

As night fell, the difficulty of the unorganized effort was compounded by darkness. There was a full moon and many of the men searched without the benefit of lights or torches. While a large area of fields and woods were scoured, there was little pattern to the search. As the moonlight waned and sporadic rain began to fall, the party grew weary and frustrated. Sometime between 2:00 and 3:00 am, plans were made to defer the search until daylight on Friday morning.

Lee Sharp, Janie's brother, was ten years older, obviously fond of his little sister and a strong supporter of his family. Eager to find her, he returned to the search alone, well before the others as daylight approached at 6:00 am that morning. He returned to Commodore Road, only about a quarter mile from the Sharp home. He immediately concentrated his efforts on an overgrown area on the west side of a path leading southeast from the Commodore Road. Leaving the trail, he followed a shallow ravine leading to a small branch of water. It was here that he found the body of his sister, Janie.

Information conflicts here. Some indicated that

upon finding the body, Lee Sharp fainted and it was several minutes before he came to and began shouting for help. In court testimony, Lee denied this but did admit to losing his composure before crying out to others who had since resumed the search.

Janie's body was partially submerged in the shallow branch in a muddy pool of water. Her throat had been slashed from ear to ear and there was evidence that she had been struck in the head with considerable force. Some reports using graphic descriptions, stated that her head indicated tremendous damage, while later testimony at trial seemed to indicate that she had been struck possibly with the butt of a pistol. There was little blood in and around the pool of water which suggested that she was killed by the blow to the head before her throat was slashed or that she had been killed elsewhere and the body placed here after her death.

Rape was a term not used in any of the news reports. Given the sensibilities of the time, its use would not have been considered appropriate. It was expected that the reader could draw their conclusions from the use of terms such as "assault" and "her person had been violated." While sexual assault was a forgone conclusion, it was never addressed specifically in the investigation and trials. Later information indicated that Dr. Clemmons told others that she had undoubtedly been the victim of rape.

Near the body were found her packages from the store, the Commercial Appeal newspaper and letters. Her parasol lay between her knees. Witnesses testified that the handkerchief that she was known to carry was not among these items.

The scene was undoubtedly gruesome and Janie's father and brother were distraught. One member of the party offered his raincoat to cover the body. But unable to bear the sight of his daughter lying in that cold muddy pool, he gathered her remains and returned the body to the family home. Upon learning of her daughter's death, Mrs. Sharp became despondent and family and neighbors feared for her health.

Calls were made and the Winston County Sheriff A.P. Hull and a group of men from the town of Louisville were headed to Rural Hill by midmorning. Because the Winston County Sheriff lacked bloodhounds, the sheriff in neighboring Attala County was contacted and by noon, a handler from the neighboring town of Kosciusko and his dog were on the scene.

Janie's body was placed on a bed in a room of the Sharp home. While not directly indicated, trial testimony indicated that several people, particularly women of the community were allowed into the room to view and attend to the body.

Throughout the morning, a crowd had gathered at the Sharp farm; many shading themselves underneath the long front gallery of the home while speculating and casting suspicious glances among themselves. Only a few doubted that the murderer was a member of the community and possibly someone present.

Questions were forming and speculations about behavior during the search, along with past conversations about Janie and her family and old grudges and loyalties were leading some to form quick opinions about one young man in the crowd.

But for now, a family was left to mourn the loss of a young, vibrant daughter. Given the heat of July and the customs of the time, Perninah Jane Sharp was to be buried the next day - Saturday, July 23, 1910 in a rural cemetery at White Hall Church just a few miles to the east. She was to lie next to her little sister who had passed away fifteen years earlier.

OBITUARY

MISS JANIE SHARP

The Memory of Miss Janie Sharp.

The 21ˢᵗ and 22 days of July 1910, was the saddest and most sorrowful days that ever came to our neighborhood and the surrounding communities in the past history.

On the afternoon of July, the 21ˢᵗ while Miss Janie Sharp was returning from the Post Office all alone, not thinking of the great and sad fate that was to be her doom, but gladly fulfilling her task of duty kind hearted and true, but alas by the hand of some foul assassin the sweet spirit of Miss Janie was forced to take its flight from loved ones and friends and world of sin and sorrow, back to God who gave this life. It was oh so sad, almost enough to freeze the blood in our veins to see where she was so brutally murdered, all alone, no loved ones or friends to come to her aid or rescue.

Little did she think that lovely afternoon while the Great light of the world was shedding his golden rays of light and bathing our lovely south land with his warm smiles, making the sweet flowers and forest look lovely and gay, that she would be taken home the next morning, a cold murdered corps, oh, how sad to know such was the case and such was her sad fate, but she passed from this earth to join the redeemed throng and sing redemptions holy song. Her sweet voice will be heard no more by those she loved and helped. She will be seen no more in the home and her place in the church is vacant, but we know where to find her, for she has gone to that happy home above, we miss her, oh, we miss her for her place in the Sunday school is vacant and oh how we miss her there for her sweet smiles and kind words always cheered us on.

She was born April 14th 1892 in Winston County near Center Ridge Church, she had lived in the Rural Hill neighborhood where she was murdered two and a half years. How this dear one is missed no one can ever know. But it should draw us all nearer to heaven to lose our loved one. If we have faith in the precious one who said, Let not your heart be troubled; ye believe in God, believe also in me. She joined the Methodist church at Rural Hill in 1908 and was a consistent and faithful member. The Funeral service was conducted by Brother T.L. Oaks at Center Ridge Church, where the sad and grief stricken family together with a large concourse of relatives and sympathying friends saw the mortal remains put to rest, there to await the happy resurrection of the kind and true. She has left her pilgrimage on earth, where she suffered the sad and awful death and gone to the house in the skies prepared for those who *loved the Lord. It is a comfort to know that she has gone to a home, where there is no suffering, no pain, no sorrow, no grief but all joy. There is rest, there is peace, there she can pluck sweet flowers from the beautiful garden of heaven and rest by the pure river of the water of life, clear as crystal proceeding out of the throne of God.*

She was a kind and true member of the Farmer's Educational and Cooperative Union of America and be it resolved that we extend our deepest heartfelt sympathy to the grief stricken father, mother, brothers and sister.

May the blessings of God wait upon them and the Sun of Glory shine around their hearts, may the gates of plenty, honor, and happiness be always open to them, may strife disturb not their days nor sorrow distress their nights; and finally may the Savior's blood wash them from all impurities and prepare them to enter into the land of everlasting felicity.

CHAPTER 3.
The Suspect

While violent deaths were not uncommon at the time, they usually involved disputes between neighbors or rivals, alcohol was often involved and there was rarely any doubt as to who the perpetrator might be. This crime was brutal and perpetrated upon a young woman, a young woman that all in the community knew well. Many were related to Janie, others attended school, church and socials with her as well. Some recalled interacting with the vivacious young woman at the recent July 4th picnic.

Many were there when her body was discovered and saw the torment of a father as he came upon that horrific scene just a few hours before. The men gathered at the Sharp home were in an ugly mood.

No one recalled any strangers in the community that could have committed this crime and there was no evidence or apparent desire to place blame upon any of the blacks in the area. Most believed that the killer had to be one of them.

Suspicions almost immediately turned to a young man named Swinton Permenter. Swinton was a teenager of similar age (not yet eighteen) as Janie and the youngest of the eight children of Edward Permenter, another local farmer who lived a half mile to the south and east of the Sharp place along what is now known as the Neal Ray Road.

The Ed Permenter family – Swinton is the young boy next to his seated father. Walton is the young man in the back row.

There are few descriptions of Swinton other than that he was tall, dark-haired and handsome. The only known photograph published at the time was a small inset image in the Commercial Appeal that presented a clean shaven, dapper young man dressed in suit and tie with a fedora perched rakishly atop a mop of curly hair. Recently, a more detailed photo of Swinton has surfaced.

It is possible that Swinton was just not well liked by
some in the community. There was talk that he
lusted after Janie, that he had even made some
crude comments in the past about his desire for her.
Some claimed that he held bad feelings toward the
family, Janie's father, in particular, because he
refused to allow Swinton to pursue Janie's
affections.

And then there was another rumor - a rumor that
was repeated in at least one newspaper in the days
after the murder that undoubtedly cast immediate
suspicion upon the young man. Swinton's
reputation was shaded by a lingering accusation of
an attempted assault upon a young girl. Reports
were that he had been suspected and even tried for
an attack (probably of a sexual nature) upon a seven
or ten-year-old child. The rumor was never fully
substantiated and the time and place were never
indicated, although the name of the young victim
was disclosed. Swinton denied the claim and no
further proof was ever presented.

Swinton's reputed behavior before, during and after
the search aroused suspicion amongst the crowd as
well. It became known that he had been at a
swimming hole with several other young men that

afternoon on Lobutcha Creek that flowed between Rural Hill and the community of Hinze to the south. At some point they separated. In the minds of some, this could have placed him near the scene of the crime in the general time frame of the murder.

When the alarm was raised that Janie was missing, almost all the able men of the community rushed to aid in the search. A pair of men went to the Permenter home and the nearby home of Swinton's uncle Ol' * (which was closest to the murder scene) in the early hours of the search to ask if anyone had seen Janie and to ask Swinton to assist. They claimed to have not found Swinton even though in later trial testimony, his sister insisted that he had returned home from the field where he had been plowing and had arrived sometime between 5:00 and 6:00 pm.

A local man, Tom McCool joined the search as darkness approached. One of the first things he did was go to the Permenter house in search of Swinton. He was not there. A short time later he encountered Swinton and his uncle Ol' Permenter about a half mile from the Permenter home walking on Commodore Road.

McCool asked "Why ain't you assisting in the search

for Janie?" Swinton seemed hesitant, stating "Well, wait until I go home and get a horse to ride and I'll go with you." McCool pointed out that he was walking and that Swinton didn't need a horse either.

After some persuasion, Swinton agreed to join him. It would be sometime around 10:00 pm before Swinton joined a group of men that included Lee Sharp along the Commodore Road.

Lee and others in the party felt that Permenter behaved strangely during the search. When several men suggested searching a particular patch of undergrowth on the west side of a side road, Swinton was reputed to say "Boys, it's no use going in there, I've hunted those woods thoroughly." This area later proved to be the location of Janie's body.

Either due to Swinton's statement or for other reasons, the area was not searched at that time and the men continued their hunt for Janie in other areas. Later that night, again according to testimony, Permenter made suggestions to search areas in the opposite direction of where the body was eventually found – "Something in my heart tells me she's back that way."

When the searchers returned the next morning after Janie's body had been found, Swinton

Permenter was in the group but others still felt his behavior was unusual. He lay down near a sapling tree away from all the other men and showed little interest until someone remarked that the law would most certainly be bringing bloodhounds to attempt to track the killer.

This statement aroused Permenter who seemed eager to let everyone know that he had been searching in those woods and that any bloodhound was likely to track his scent as well as the killer's. He repeated a similar statement later in the morning at the Sharp home.

After following the crowd of men to the Sharp home and as they awaited the arrival of Sheriff Hull, Swinton left with another man, Terrell Hall, and returned to his home.

Suggs waited outside in the yard for a coat he had asked to borrow from Swinton. He observed Swinton come to the porch with a pan of water, wash himself and enter a side room of the home where he changed clothes and shoes. Suggs and Swinton's father walked back to the Sharp home and Swinton later returned to the Sharp's with other family members in a wagon.

The crowd around the Sharp home had been building throughout the morning as the news of

Janie's death spread. Talk continued not only about Swinton Permenter but two other young men were viewed with suspicion as well. Alonzo Burchfield and Walter Cummings had been at that swimming hole with Swinton on the previous afternoon. Their association with Permenter and the fact that they were each other's alibi did not sit well with some.

There is no direct eyewitness information about the mood and attitude of the crowd during those hours. Folks gathered in the yard and about the house and it was likely that the community had already begun to separate themselves into two camps – those who had faith in Swinton and those who cast a suspicious eye his way.

Upon arrival, the sheriff and his men visited the crime scene and took what evidence they could find. Given the activities of the search party from the previous night, the crowd that had gathered around the crime scene and the removal of Janie's body, some evidence would have certainly been lost or jumbled.

A local Justice of the Peace named R.B. McAlilly was present prior to the removal of the body and he asked Dr. Clemmons to examine Janie's corpse. Clemmons later provided a description of the position of the body and the nature of her wounds to the Sheriff at the scene.

Janie had been struck in the head with a blunt object, possibly the butt of a pistol. It was a horrific blow and likely caused her death. The killer then cut her throat from ear to ear and it appeared that she had been stabbed several times under the chin in an attempt to assure her death.

A number of shoe prints were also discovered. Some were obviously those of Janie but others were surmised to be those of the killer. A deputy cut a witch hazel stick and used it to measure the length of the male's print.

There was never any information or testimony concerning the crime scene directly or if the actions of the searchers might have contaminated any evidence. No evidence was ever submitted to confirm that the prints were actually those of the killer and not of someone else who had been at the scene. Given the chaotic nature of the previous night's search, any footprint evidence would be questionable.

By noon, the sheriff from Attala County and J.T. Hanna, the dog handler from Kosciusko had arrived with a hound named Ruth Hindoo. Hanna claimed to be a third-generation dog trainer and he had faith in the dog's ability. Others were not so sure, given the dog's young age of only fourteen months.

Hanna started the dog where Janie's body was found. The dog tracked north up the branch about forty yards and along the east side of the branch. Here Hanna and the sheriff noted an area where the ground was scuffed. The dog moved away from the branch in a southeasterly direction and the party observed several sets of footprints at different locations. The prints on at least two separate occasions were determined to be both a man's and a woman's.

Ruth Hindoo continued tracking south and approached the farm of Ed Permenter. As the dog reached the yard, Hanna checked her at the gate but soon released her again. She moved away from the house and out into the road where she scented a group of men and then returned to the house and barn lot. She trailed the scent around the lot, the stable and the barn and returned to the front gate and reared upon it.

At this point, Ed Permenter, Swinton's father met them at the gate and Walter Permenter, Swinton's older brother appeared on the porch of the house with a gun in his hand. Hanna later testified that he believed that Walter wanted to shoot him or the dog.

The dog returned to a group of five men standing nearby. In the center was Swinton Permenter. According to reports, the dog looked at him, threw his head around to his trainer and scented Swinton.

This was enough for Sheriff Hull. Knowing that Swinton had returned home and changed clothes, a search was made to find them. Upon entering the side room, they found the clothes he had worn previously and, in a pocket, - a Barlow knife, a piece of tobacco and two handkerchiefs- a man's and a woman's. Based upon the dog's behavior and the suspicion of the origin of the woman's handkerchief, Swinton Permenter was taken into custody as the primary suspect in the murder of Janie Sharp.

O.L. Permenter was often referred to as Ol' Permenter

Swinton Permenter

Published in Commercial Appeal at time of 2nd trial

Provided by family members

CHAPTER 4.
No Trial Needed

By the time the bloodhound, Ruth Hindoo, had trailed the scent to the Permenter home and directly scented Swinton, the crowd gathered was slowly but surely turning into a mob. Many were convinced of Permenter's guilt and there were rumblings that a trial was not necessary and the matter could be taken care of right then and there. Emotions were high due to the horrible nature of the crime and its proximity. The victim was a young woman and one of their own.

There is evidence that at least one local man visited several homesteads during the afternoon asking men to join a mob, claiming that they had a hundred armed men and were ready to take Swinton.

Another report indicated that either on the night of the search or the following day, Hewlett Ray had stated that if the suspicion against Permenter got any stronger – "he would shoot the devil out of him."

Sheriff Hull and the men he had brought with him from outside of the community began to believe that a lynching was a real possibility and feared that they could not control the crowd of men. By whatever means available, probably from the Permenter home, Hull telephoned back to Louisville and urgently requested more men in case things got out of hand.

Hull quickly took Swinton into custody along with two other young men, Alonzo Burchfield and Walter Cummings, who had been with Permenter at the swimming hole on Lobutcha Creek on the afternoon of the murder.

They began the long fourteen-mile journey along what is now known as State Highway 14 - back to Louisville and the jail at the Winston County Courthouse in the center of town - an angry mob of roughly seventy-five men trailing behind. The additional men requested by the sheriff met them along the way.

Tensions did not ease upon their arrival in Louisville. The men from Rural Hill were quickly joined by an ever-growing crowd of locals outside the courthouse throughout the afternoon and into the evening. Anger grew as rumors spread and agitators took full advantage of the opportunity to rouse the crowd. Later newspaper reports *(Winston County Journal and numerous others)* indicated that talk of lynching the suspects was circulating throughout the day.

Responsible parties (likely including the Circuit Court Judge, George A. McLean, who happened to be in town for a session) feared the worst. After some discussion, the decision was made to get the suspects out of town for their safety.

At 11:00 pm on Friday, July 22, Permenter, Burchfield and Cummings were taken to the depot a few blocks from the Courthouse in Louisville and placed on a train procured for the sole purpose of the suspects' transport to Winona, Mississippi.

Roughly forty-five miles to the north, Winona was chosen for several reasons. It was far enough away to ease the tensions, it was easy access by train and most importantly, it was the home of Judge McLean, the 5th Circuit Judge, who would likely preside over the case and any grand jury indictment.

Permenter's clothing and the items found in his pockets were held as evidence. The woman's handkerchief was particularly damning. Newspaper reports were the only record of the handling of the evidence and the accuracy of information was suspect. The Winston County Journal indicated that the clothes appeared to have been washed but that there was evidence of blood on some of the clothing. *This was contradictory to the statements made by Terrell Suggs who saw Swinton change clothes after the search.*

The Journal also reported that the County Attorney, J. B. Gully had taken the items to Mississippi A&M College (now Mississippi State University) located in Starkville, thirty miles to the northeast, to be analyzed with a chemical test to determine if any blood was human in nature. *This blood evidence, as can best be determined, was not presented at trial. Based on the lack of further reports, it is likely that no blood was found or the results were indeterminant.*

Over the next few days and weeks, newspaper reports began to sensationalize the event. In modern terms, the story went viral and appeared in papers as far away as the West Coast, New York and all over the South.

Many reports were inaccurate and assuredly based on hearsay information. Timelines were inaccurate, names and ages of the parties involved were also inaccurately reported. Speculation as to the nature of Swinton's and Janie's relationship were reported as fact and the lynching threat was almost certainly exaggerated.

By Saturday morning, July 23, Permenter,

Burchfield and Cummings were safely tucked away
in jail in Montgomery County. Permenter was
considered the main suspect and it is likely that
Burchfield and Cummings were being held to
guarantee their safety and to possibly elicit
testimony.

Walter Permenter believed in the innocence of his
younger brother as strongly as Lee Sharp believed
in his guilt. Walter began asking questions and
taking notes in an attempt to prove Swinton had
nothing to do with the murder. One note indicated
that he believed that the County Attorney, Jim
Gully carried Swinton's clothes to Winona in an
attempt to sway his testimony - "*told Alonzo
Burchfield various reports for facts and persuaded
him to say that he believed Swinton guilty. Reports
said that it had been proved that he did no
plowing. There was blood on his clothes.*"

In a strange twist, Walter also recorded evidence of
bruises on Swinton's chest but this was apparently
never brought up in trial or presented in any other
news reports or documentation. The note reads as
follows: "*Swinton and Dillard were boxing in the
store and Swinton got some bruises on his breast.
Were noticed by boys at the creek. Levi made
mention of sand at creek.*" This was likely an
attempt to prove that no bruises were present

before Janie's murder.

The Sharp family was in mourning. The condition of the body and the summer heat led the family to arrange Janie's funeral on Saturday as well. Janie's younger sister, Nellie Lenora who had passed fifteen years earlier had been interred at the cemetery at Center Ridge Methodist Church located just a few miles to the east of Rural Hill and Janie was placed beside her.

The following photo of the Sharp family is believed be taken just a few hours after the funeral.

The Sharp family – possibly taken on July 23, 1910 – the day of Janie's funeral. Bottom row: Cleveland Sharp, Will Sharp-Janie's father, Hazel, Martha-Janie's mother, Lee Sharp. Top Row: Lena, Zora, Wes Morgan

& baby Mamie, Mae Morgan, Willie, Nathan

Lee Sharp, Janie's older brother was convinced of Swinton Permenter's guilt and made every effort to prove it and convince others. That afternoon after his sister's funeral, he returned to the scene of the crime looking for further evidence. While not attributed to Lee Sharp, the Winston County Journal reported on July 29, 1910, information that likely was relayed by him and may or may not have been confirmed later by the Sheriff:

Tracks were found leading from the road to Cyrus Ray's home that led into the nearby woods and down a branch. It was speculated that the initial assault occurred here as Janie turned off Commodore Road and headed for her uncle's home. It appeared that Janie escaped her attacker and ran for a few yards before she was caught again. She escaped a second time and ran farther before being overtaken again where evidence of a major struggle could be seen. It was believed that she escaped for a third time as she ran back toward the road before her attacker caught her one last time and struck her with the blow that took her life.

It was never clear if this location was the spot where her body was found or if the killer moved the body into the branch and the pool of water in an attempt to hide it or destroy evidence.

There is also no evidence that the sheriff returned to the scene for further investigation or to verify the above statement. It may well be that he believed that it was not necessary. Forensic science was unheard of in 1910, he had a suspect in custody and likely believed that a confession was just a matter of time.

Regardless of who was responsible, Janie had apparently put up a strong struggle for her life. For now, a suspect was in custody and it appeared that most, including law enforcement, were convinced that seventeen-year-old Swinton Permenter was guilty of the crime.

CHAPTER 5.
First Trial

Little is known about the activities of the next few days. No documentation related to the sheriff's investigation exists but it is likely that time was spent in and around the Rural Hill community gathering details, interviewing anyone who might have any information about the crime and gathering information about Swinton Permenter, Walter Cummings and Alonzo Burchfield.

It was reported that a deputy from Winston County traveled to Winona and spoke with Alonzo Burchfield and Walter Cummings in an attempt to solicit testimony against Swinton. Further information would suggest that it was actually the county attorney, J.B Gully, who made the journey to Winona. This would corroborate Walter Permenter's notes. It would be Wednesday of the following week before Sheriff Hull interviewed the three boys.

In another unresolved twist to the case, The Kosciusko Star Ledger in neighboring Attala County reported that on July 25th, the Monday after the murder, a fourth man had been arrested in the case. This report was confusing and not substantiated by any other papers. No details were provided and the man's name was listed as Charley Horn in the body of the report but listed as Charlie Lake in the headline. It appears that no other newspapers picked up on this story. This arrest was not mentioned in later trial testimony and it is likely that this individual may have simply been sought and questioned as a witness in the case or was just a case of unsubstantiated rumor reported as fact.

Any investigation was likely complicated by the bloodthirsty mood that pervaded the community. Much energy and effort were expended in calming those who were calling for immediate justice and there was certainly pressure upon law enforcement to lean toward Swinton as the killer.

There were some reports that Judge McLean spoke to the mob of men gathered at the courthouse at the time of the arrests and assured them that a speedy trial would take place. It became apparent that some felt that a jury should be immediately empaneled.

When McLean later adjourned the court session already in place and returned to his home in Winona, some felt betrayed and let it be known that if a trial did not take place soon, they would take matters into their own hands. Over time, cooler heads prevailed in the community. Will Sharp was credited with doing much to calm the situation.

Rumors continued to multiply and tensions between families and neighbors were high. Some came to the defense of the young man, Swinton Permenter. Others would have likely killed him on sight.

As in any small community, the murder and suspects were the only topic of conversation around the dinner table, at the post offices, country stores and front porches as neighbors visited neighbors. As the Sharp's had many family ties in the immediate area and goaded on by Lee Sharp, most were quick to believe in Swinton's guilt.

One man said he believed Swinton guilty because who else could it be. Another said that "even if he had information to clear Swinton, he would not tell it because he didn't like Ed Permenter who had had some lies on him."

Others believed that the case against Swinton was not so clear cut. Some felt that the dog was not reliable and was prevented from trailing further or had even been led to scent Swinton. Another claimed to have seen something done with Swinton's clothes after they were collected as evidence, but it was something he would not tell.

Still another claimed that there were two sets of male tracks found alongside Janie's – indicating that two men were involved.

Regardless of all the rumors and idle talk, three young men were in custody but the early evidence seemed to show that only one man committed the crime and most believed that man was Swinton Permenter. Suspicions about Burchfield and Cummings began to wane.

There was a significant amount of circumstantial evidence against Swinton:

A handkerchief believed to be the victim's was found in Permenter's possession. The Sharp family confirmed that the handkerchief found in Swinton's pocket belonged to Janie. She was known to have it in her possession before the murder and it was missing from the crime scene.

The tracks found at the murder scene were a close match to Permenter's shoe size. A sheriff's deputy had cut a stick to measure the track and it would be submitted as evidence.

His general proximity to the area and time of the crime did not exclude him. This was likely the reason that Cummings and Burchfield were taken into custody as well.

The bloodhound tracked from the crime scene to the Permenter home and at least according to some, seemed to specifically scent upon Swinton.

His strange and, at least to some, misleading behavior during the search for Janie was suspicious.

There were rumors also. Some claimed that Swinton Permenter made some remarks indicating his desire for Janie's affection and that he had made some vague threats against Janie's father, possibly because Will Sharp did not approve of Permenter.

This circumstantial evidence against this young man was significant - if it was accurate. But there were also gaps and questions in the evidence or at least in the investigation:

Permenter's clothes had been submitted to a nearby college for examination of blood evidence. An official report had not been completed. While a witness observed him washing on the morning after the murder, there was no clear evidence presented to show that his clothing had been washed.

Based upon Lee Sharp's observations, Janie put up a significant struggle for her life. This could have resulted in marks, bruises or scratches upon the killer. Despite Walter Permenter's notes, none were ever referenced on Permenter.

Some reported that Permenter was carrying a pistol on the night of the search. This would seem significant given that it was speculated that the blow to Janie's head may have been from the butt of a pistol. The weapon was never mentioned again in trial testimony.

There was also no mention of a knife. Janie's throat had been cut from ear to ear and apparently stabbed as well. Other than a small Barlow knife in Swinton's pocket, a knife was never recovered or submitted into evidence nor was there any indication that Permenter's knife had been examined for traces of blood.

****

Newspaper reports were muddled. The Winston County Journal, the Kosciusko Star Ledger, Kosciusko Herald and the Jackson Daily printed detailed reports on the crime but tended to sensationalize the events and at least one clearly stated a belief in not only Permenter's guilt but that of Burchfield and Cummings as well. One reported that Circuit Judge George A. McLean had recessed court and attended the scene of the crime with the sheriff. This was never verified but was a possibility due to the fact that McLean was in Louisville presiding over a grand jury at the time of the murder.

On Wednesday following the murder, Sheriff Hull caught the train to Winona to personally interview the suspects and confer with Judge McLean. He returned later that day with Walter Cummings and Alonzo Burchfield. There was no straightforward evidence connecting them to the crime and the sheriff believed that it was safe to allow them to return to their homes.

Walter Cummings was released unconditionally while Burchfield was released under bond requiring him to appear before an upcoming grand jury. The opinion was that he would be a significant material witness in the case. Swinton Permenter remained in a Montgomery County jail until his trial.

Permenter had his supporters. Funds were raised from family and friends to pay for his defense, attorneys were hired and they prepared for the biggest trial ever held in Winston County. Permenter was not released on bond and there was little for him to do but consult with his lawyers from his jail cell as the days dragged on during a long hot

Mississippi summer.

Even in 1910, the legal process was deliberate. It would be nearly two months before another grand jury could be convened. Without effort, it could have taken much longer. In this, Swinton was fortunate. Judge McLean made good on his promise to speed the process when he called for a special grand jury on September 8th and set the date for September 19th for the main purpose of an indictment of Swinton Permenter.

Several cases were heard during the grand jury session but on the morning of September 19, 1910, Swinton Permenter appeared before Judge McLean in a Winston County courtroom.

No detailed court records exist of this event. Court minutes only provide the results of any decision. Twenty citizens had been selected to serve as grand jurors earlier in the month. The names of many of these jurors are still common names across the county. A.H. Halfacre was the foreman and others included: Barnhill, Cooper, Pearson, Kelly, Holmes, Moore, Spence, Dawson, Pope (2), Clay, Kinard, Dempsey, Tisdale, Taggart, Roberson, Boyd, Price and Miller.

The Circuit Court minutes read: *The State of Mississippi vs Swinton Permenter: charge of murder. This day came the District Attorney who prosecutes for the State and the defendant Swinton Permenter in his own proper person and being represented by counsel and being arraigned on a bill of indictment charging him with murder, pleads not guilty therefore the Court remanded him to jail.*

The Permenter family felt that Swinton was being railroaded. Lies were being told and testimony twisted, possibly by intimidation. Walter Permenter believed that one of the boys with Swinton was being pressured to change the time when the boys separated. He also noted that at least one man indicated that if a detective who had become involved in the case, Ben Walker, took Swinton's side too much on the stand that they would "put him out from there."

Contrary to modern day criminal trials, things advanced quickly. There would be no change of venue. The trial was set in Louisville in early October, 1910. The case was to be heard before Judge George A. McLean with prosecutors, Lamb, Gully and Jones and local defense attorneys, Rodgers, Brantley, and Hopkins.

A postcard of downtown Louisville dated 1909. The courthouse can be seen in the middle right of the image

The trial began on October 3 as the defense immediately asked for a change of venue. This request was promptly denied by Judge McLean and jury selection began that morning. A pool of 126 potential jurors was determinedly accepted or rejected until a final jury of twelve was seated. Again, the names of jurors still reflect the families of current residents of the community. Some names in the court record are almost indiscernible. The jury consisted of:

Jim Ming, J.W. Edwards, Ike Yarbrough, Calvin

Palmer, J. O. Landrum, M. H. Hanna, Printis (Prentiss) Adcock, A.L. Jackson, H.O. Houston, Frank Hindman, J.A. Hatcher, D.C. Coleman

L. to R sitting: Sheriff A.P. Hull, James Ming, Calvin Palmer, J.A. Hatcher, M.H. Hannah, J.O. Landrum, H.O. Houston, L. to R standing Bailiffs: W.H. Lovorn & C.A. Jones, Prentiss Adcock, A.L. Jackson, Ike Yarbrough, Frank Hindman, J.W. Edwards, D.C. Coleman, Bailiffs: W.E. Murphy & J.W. Triplett

Photo of 1st Jury in Winston County
Possibly taken by Commercial Appeal

Because of the spectacular nature of the crime and the bad blood that had developed, Judge McLean empaneled four special bailiffs for the trial and jury: W. H Lavon, C. A. Jones, W.E. Murphy and J. W. Triplett.

It is unfortunate that no transcript of the trial has survived - at least not one that can be found. The only written information available are the court minutes, limited newspaper articles and some references in a later Mississippi Supreme Court ruling. Circuit court records were maintained locally and were not archived at the state level. At least one courthouse demolition and new construction and countless circuit clerks have committed any records to the dust of history.

While there are no records of testimony, there is an extensive witness list that includes as many as sixty-eight called to testify. These include many familiar names: Sharp, Ray, Burchfield, McCool, Shumaker, Steed, Horn and McLeod to name a few. It is interesting to note that none of Swinton Permenter's immediate family was included in this list.

One name not on the witness list was a man named Ben (referred to as Hugh or Dan in some newspaper reports) Walker. Walker was reputed to be from the Mississippi Delta, possibly from the Cleveland area and presented himself as a private detective. He had been known to be in the area shortly after the murder and it is a reasonable assumption that he was hired by the Permenter family to investigate the case and find the guilty party. On at least one occasion, Walker insinuated that he had actually been hired by the Governor of Mississippi, Edmond

Noel, to work the case due to its volatile nature.

(The Noel name would surface again in 1954 in nearby Holmes County as Eddie Noel, a mixed-race man and nephew of Edmond Noel was the subject of one of the largest and most bungled manhunts ever in Mississippi for the killing of a white bar owner.)

There is no physical description of Walker, no reference to his age or qualifications as a detective, no background or family connections. Unknown to the community, he did not make a good impression or win friends. While not included on the witness list, there is strong evidence that he did testify in the trial but had little of consequence to say and made a poor impression upon the jury.

The trial began on a Monday and the verdict was reached on the Tuesday of the following week. Court was held on Saturday. Jury selection encompassed much of the first day, October 3 and summations filled the last day, October 11.

The trial was likely the biggest event seen in Winston County since Grierson's Raid during the Civil War. The courtroom was packed and included a number of women which was highly unusual at that time in history.

****

The trial produced one unusual and humorous story passed through the generations of a family. I was told this story by a local woman who indicated that her mother was eight years old at the time of the murder. Her grandfather attended the trial and allowed his two daughters to play in the hallway while he was in the courtroom.

The two girls found the lady's bathroom and having never seen an indoor toilet, they were fascinated. The water tank was suspended above the toilet and as curiosity got the best of them, one of them pulled the flush chain. When the water began to flow, they feared that they had broken something. One held the other up to look inside the tank and discovered that lifting the float stopped the flow of water. One of the girls tore a strip off her petticoat and tied the float up and then scampered out.

****

On the final day of the trial, the courtroom was packed again. Men blocked the aisles and sat in the window wells of the room. Swinton's mother had not attended the trial until the last day when she sat beside her son.

At 9:00 am, the prosecution began its closing arguments. An ex-District Attorney Jones spoke for an hour and urged the jury to perform their duty for Winston County and the State of Mississippi, stating that the physical evidence told the truth in the case and vilifying Permenter in the process.

The defense's statement was conducted by the local Attorney Hopkins who argued that the prosecution had not proved its case or presented a reasonable motive for the crime.

By the afternoon at 1:45 pm on Tuesday, October 11, the case was handed to the jury.

The decision was quickly reached. Over the years, some reported that the jury returned with their verdict in as little as four minutes. This is not accurate. While jurors indicated that the decision was reached on the first ballot, it was 6:00 pm before the jury returned to the courtroom.

Recognizing the ugly mood that pervaded the community, Judge McLean cleared the courtroom before the verdict was read. The jury's decision was passed to the court clerk who read:

We, the jury, find the defendant guilty as charged of the indictment."

In less than three months, Swinton Permenter had

been arrested, tried and found guilty of the crime of murder upon Perninah Janie Sharp of Rural Hill Mississippi. There was little doubt that the rush to judgment, the mood of the community and the fear of possible retribution had considerable influence on the jury.

The Winston County Journal made much of Swinton Permenter's calm and composure throughout the trial and speculated that this worked against him in the minds of the jury.

"Permenter shows composure and nerve unknown to history, if he is normal and sane as his friends claim he is. During the ten* long days of his trial he sat with perfect composure and stolid indifference, even to the sentence of death. He seemed the least concerned of any in the room, this indifference appearance was so noticeable that it really made the case against him."

Swinton was returned to his cell in the Winston County jail overnight for sentencing the next day. A guard reported to the newspaper that Permenter broke down after the verdict but soon fell asleep.

On the morning of October 12, a request by Permenter's attorneys for a new trial was denied by Judge McLean. Before passing sentence, Judge McLean asked Permenter if he had anything to say.

An emphatic "I AM NOT GUILTY" was his only response.

Based upon the nature and severity of the crime, the sentence was a forgone conclusion. Swinton Permenter was sentenced to hang on November 25, 1910. Gallows were to be constructed by order of the county supervisors for that purpose.

This is incorrect as the trial actually lasted nine days.

CHAPTER 6.
The Appeal

An appeal of Swinton Permenter's conviction was immediately begun for presentation to the Mississippi State Supreme Court in Jackson. With an appeal before the court, his November 25 execution was on hold and the gallows construction never took place. In the meantime, due to the heightened emotions and fear for his safety, Swinton was moved out of the county.

By the 1900's, Mississippi was in the process of adding much needed prison facilities in Rankin County and Sunflower County. In 1903, the original state prison known as "The Walls" was torn down to make room for the new State Capitol Building that was constructed on the site in the center of Jackson.

In 1900, the Parchman Plantation in Sunflower County was purchased and was operating by 1905 in the Mississippi Delta. The Rankin Prison Farm was also operational by 1910 near Jackson. It is now the site of the Mississippi State Hospital Psychiatric Facility known to most Mississippians as Whitfield.

Because Swinton's case was under consideration for

appeal, he never experienced the hospitality of any of these long-term facilities. He was to spend the next few months at the Hinds County Jail in Jackson.

Swinton had become a celebrity of sort. The case and trial had been reported all over the country and the public wanted to know more about the handsome young man convicted of such a brutal murder. At least one newspaper, The Jackson Daily News, sought out information from guards and prisoners concerning Permenter.

According to an article published on November 15, 1910, Swinton was making a positive impression upon his jailers and fellow prisoners as well. His "quiet gentlemanly conduct" seemed to win over most to the belief that he was innocent of murder and a victim of circumstance. His jailers spoke highly of him and were quoted extensively in the Jackson Daily article:

"His sleep is never troubled and if this boy is guilty of the crime for which he has been condemned, he is the coldest hearted villain I ever saw. There has never been any act or word- sleeping or waking to indicate him guilty of this murder."

"The only thing that seems to bother him is his father and mother. He writes home nearly every

*day telling them he is getting along as well as can
be expected, but these letters never touch upon the
crime for which he is convicted of, except to ask
what is being done to trace the murderers of Janie
Sharp."*

*"Permenter is a jovial sort of boy but his
confinement is telling on him to some extent. He
sleeps about twelve hours at night and is gaining
weight but he does not look as well as when he
came here. I have been to his cell at night and have
never found him awake, he sleeps sound and when
he awakes in the morning, he seems refreshed and
fit for hard work."*

*"He has discussed the murder of Janie Sharp with
me some, as he has with everyone who visits him,
but has never said anything that could be
construed into even an intimation that he
committed the crime. He has, on the contrary said
he believed two other fellows committed the crime
and these two men from what I understand were
active in the prosecution.... He seems to think
everything will turn out right in the end and I
believe it will."*

Swinton would spend the winter of 1910-1911 in the
Hinds County Jail and it would be spring before the
Mississippi Supreme Court ruled on his case.

In the meantime, things were returning to some level of calm in Winston County and around Rural Hill. Ben Walker had been hired at the behest of the Permenter family. Funds were pooled and it is likely that Elbert Vowell, an uncle of Swinton's paid much of the cost.

The self- proclaimed private investigator seemed to make little or no progress in the case and was not making a good impression around the area. Many believed that he was simply biding his time and bleeding the family and supporters financially until their money ran out.

There are no records of his investigation and no witnesses to explain his activities. Many believed that Walter Permenter, Swinton's older brother, was a confidante of Walker and knew much about the investigation of the case.

The stress of the murder had a major impact on the Sharp family and Mrs. Sharp, Janie's mother, was devastated. The family or at least Mrs. Sharp and the younger children, left Rural Hill on October 18, 1910 and returned to the community of McCool in neighboring Choctaw County, a few miles distant from their farm and the scene of the crime. McCool was a fairly new community that had developed around the railroad depot established in 1883.

Apparently, the family had lived in or near the little town prior to moving to Rural Hill.

Sometime after that move, Mrs. Sharp published an open letter (in the Winston County Journal) to the community. It is interesting to note that in the letter, there was a glaring inconsistency that would not be expected from a mother writing about her own child. Janie's name was spelled differently than is shown on public records and on her tombstone. It seems likely that while Mrs. Sharp may have dictated the letter, someone outside of the family wrote the document based on this inaccuracy. It is presented here without editing:

LETTERS WERE A COMFORT

Dear Mrs. Gray and All the Kind Sisters-Here comes a broken-hearted mother. Sisters, I want to thank each and everyone who sent me letters and I am sorry I can't answer all personally. Please remember I appreciate them just as if I had answered them all. They were so sweet and sympathizing, but dear people, it sometimes seems like my trouble is more than I can bear. Oh, I miss my dear, sweet Jannie ever so much. It's awful to think she had to die like she did, but thank God, she was a pure, sweet girl and I know she is now quietly resting with God. The one sweet consolation I have is I can meet my dear child, and I know I have two sweet angels in heaven. One little babe, three months and three days old died fifteen years ago. I thought that was trouble, but sisters, no one knows what trouble is until they have a child to walk off well and hearty and be brought back murdered as my child was. Dear sisters, after my dear child had suffered this awful death, she had one of the sweetest smiles on her dear face and looked like she wanted to tell me all about it. Oh, how I wish she could have told me all about it, but God knows best, and all will be explained someday. Oh, our home is so lonely without Jannie. She was so lively and industrious. She did most all of the housework and cut and did all of the sewing. We surely miss her very much. She was always singing and playing the organ every spare moment, and she was the only grown child I had at home. I have three little children at home now, a boy 14, a girl 11 and one 9, but they are all in school and I will be so lonely. My oldest daughter, whose home is in Oklahoma, has been with us; came very soon after Jannie was taken, but will leave for home tomorrow, and we will miss her and her two sweet little boys. She says she intends to write a letter to the Commercial Appeal when she gets home. I have two married sons, living twelve miles away and another daughter married and living eight miles from me. She has a dear little ten-month old girl and she will spend next week with me and help me get my fall sewing done. Well, we have moved back to our old home, which is in the pretty little town of McCool. We moved Oct. 18, but I left some good, dear friends around Rural Hill and they were so good and kind to us in our great trouble and we can never forget their kindness. We have friends here, too and from the good letters I received, I know I have sympathizing friends all over the states.

Mrs. Carrie Carter of Plattsburg, Miss., was so thoughtful and kind in asking you, sisters to write me and your good words have relieved me of many sad hours. Well, I will bid you all adieu for this time with best wishes for all and our dear paper, I am.

Mrs. Will Sharp

*****

On April 24, 1911, The Supreme Court of
Mississippi "reversed and remanded" the verdict
issued by the jury in Louisville on October 11 of the
previous year against Swinton Permenter. The
ruling was primarily based upon flaws in the
instructions provided to the jury concerning the
application of circumstantial evidence and the
concept of reasonable doubt.

After providing a brief synopsis of the initial trial,
the court ruled that an instruction given to the
jurors was "fatally erroneous." Jurors were
instructed that the defendant could be convicted if
circumstantial evidence generates full conviction in
their mind beyond a reasonable doubt. The
Supreme Court held that "full conviction" is not the
criteria or degree of proof necessary to convict.

Citing other cases, the court held that
circumstantial evidence must be weighed with
caution and that every other theory except for the
guilt of a defendant must be excluded by that
evidence.

The Supreme Court held that proper instruction as
requested by the appellant was refused related to
the weighing of circumstantial evidence and that
the jury should have been informed that any fact
proven to their satisfaction which was inconsistent

with the defendant's guilt constituted reasonable doubt.

In the ruling to reverse and remand, the Supreme Court made the following statement:

The appellant, Swinton Permenter, was convicted of murder and sentenced to hang, and appeals to this court. He was convicted on evidence wholly circumstantial, made up of many different facts and circumstances. There is grave doubt, from the record in this case of appellant's guilt.

Recognizing that this case would likely be tried again, the court refused further comment.

Considering this ruling and the time he had already spent in jail, Permenter would be eligible for bail. On Monday, May 22, 1911, Swinton Permenter was granted bail if a $10,000 bond was posted. By Tuesday, friends and family had raised sufficient funds to make the bond and Swinton was released from the Hinds County Jail on Wednesday. His brother, Walter, was in Jackson at the time and wrote the following postcard to his wife:

Dear Madie: How I would like to know how you

and babies are getting on. Guess I will be home
Wed night, though it may be later. We got Bond.
$10,000. This is the first card I ever bought or
sent. Much love and a bushel of kisses. Walton

Swinton's case would go back to Winston County
for a retrial, but a change of venue due to all the
publicity was quickly granted and the next trial
would be held in the City of Winona in Montgomery
County, the place where he had been incarcerated
prior to the first trial.

This second trial was scheduled for October, 1911.
There is no record of events during that long
summer of 1911. Swinton's whereabouts during this
time were never disclosed or discussed although it
is highly likely that he did not remain in Rural Hill
with his parents. Given the bad feelings and threats,
his safety would have certainly been in question.
With large extended families that were common at
that time, it is likely that he resided with a family
member, possibly his sister and brother-in-law in
the small town of Eupora, just a short distance from
Winona.

On the first day of the second trial in 1911, the
defense team filed for a continuance due to the
absence of several key witnesses for the defense.
Reports were that at least five defense witnesses

were not present, the key witness being Swinton's sister who was reported gravely ill and unable to testify. Over strong objections by the state, the court ruled to continue the case until its next session in April, 1912.

It would actually be August, 1912 before the final trial of Swinton Permenter, more than two years after the murder of Janie Sharp.

The events between the October continuance and the final trial only added to the tragedy and mystery surrounding the whole case.

Two additional unsolved murders, possible alternative suspects and bribery charges created doubts, distrust and served to widen the breach between those convinced of Permenter's guilt and those who supported him.

CHAPTER 7.
Ben Walker

Bad blood ruled the Rural Hill community throughout the remainder of 1911 and well into 1912 prior to the final trial. The Sharps and the Permenters both had large extended families not only in Rural Hill but in the surrounding areas. Friends and neighbors took sides based upon their connections and loyalties.

Lee Sharp, Janie's older brother was adamant that Swinton Permenter was the man who took his sister's life and felt that some – including Swinton's family members knew more than they had revealed about the case and he had no problem making his feelings public.

The Permenter family was just as strong in their convictions and apparently continued to pay Detective Ben Walker to investigate the case. Money was an obvious problem for the family – between legal fees, bond and the services of Walker, the costs were more than the family could bear alone. Some evidence exists that Elbert Vowell, Swinton's uncle, may have assisted with his bond and almost certainly paid for the bulk of Walker's fees, including room and board. It was also reported that H. B Tabor, a local businessman and employer of Walter Permenter provided funds for the defense.

The Permenters hoped that Walker would find some evidence to clear Swinton or to at least find any evidence providing an alternate theory or suspect that would weaken any case against Swinton.

Little is known about Ben Walker. There is no known physical description or reference to his age. His qualifications as an investigator, exactly where he came from and how he became involved in the Janie Sharp affair are unclear, but his short role in the case was mysterious, confounding and tragic.

A descendent of Elbert Vowell indicates that Ben Walker lived with the family and represented himself as a "Pinkerton Man." He claimed to be from the Cleveland, Ms. area but the family suspected that Walker was not his real name.

This is a real possibility as there seems to be no historical record for Walker. A later newspaper report indicated that Walker was engaged to a young lady from a prominent family in the Rural Hill area. There is no record of who that might be and an engagement has never been corroborated.

Some records (Commercial Appeal) indicate that Ben Walker testified in the first Permenter trial. This is corroborated to some degree by Walter

Permenter's notes. If accurate, in his testimony he claimed to be from Cleveland, Ms. and was "instructed" by the Governor to make inquiries into the crime. The newspaper story indicated that Walker's testimony was inconsequential and that he left a poor impression upon the court.

Most accounts indicate that Walker was actually hired by the Permenter family. He may have misrepresented himself under oath about his official status or he was later hired by the family in a non-official capacity.

Walker spent considerable time in the area while investigating the case. The distrust of outsiders and his activities on behalf of the Permenters did little to endear him to the general population in and around Rural Hill.

***

In November, 1911, a little over a year after the first trial and a month after the second trial had been delayed, Detective Ben Walker created a stir in the community when he returned from Greenville, Texas with Thomas McElroy and his family. Walker "arrested" McElroy for the murder of Janie Sharp.

McElroy was a young family man and was a

previous resident of Rural Hill and strangely enough, a son-in-law to Cyrus Ray (the uncle and neighbor of Janie). He and his family had moved to Texas in September, 1910, shortly after Janie's murder. McElroy had been a member of the search party on the day of Janie's murder. No suspicion had been cast upon McElroy prior to this time and his arrest by Walker was met with a great deal of skepticism.

It was apparent that McElroy returned to Mississippi of his own free will. In fact, his wife and two small children accompanied him and Ben Walker on the train ride from Texas. *(There is some conflicting information here as cemetery records indicate that McElroy's only child died as an infant. This is likely incorrect as other records indicate that he had a young son and daughter.)* The whole party spent the night at a Jackson hotel before catching a train to McCool and arriving at Cyrus Ray's home late in the evening on Monday, November 13. A Greenville newspaper covered the "arrest" and trip from Texas but seemed to cast doubt upon any evidence of McElroy's involvement in the murder.

"Walker has not disclosed a word of evidence to anyone. Many believe he has no tangible evidence and think he has mistaken suspicion for proof. It is true that McElroy lived within a mile or less of the scene of the crime; and it is true that he moved to

Texas soon thereafter., these, in so far as the public knows, are the only suspicious circumstances, if they rise to the dignity of such."

The facts are not directly known and no evidence was disclosed or published connecting McElroy to the crime. It is possible that Walker concocted a story that cast suspicion on McElroy to create doubt in the mind of potential jurors but there is also evidence that key witnesses against McElroy refused to testify.

McElroy seemed to have no ill will toward Walker and even encouraged his father-in-law, Cyrus Ray, to treat Walker right as he had treated him and his family properly on their trip from Texas.

Upon returning to Rural Hill and depositing the McElroy family with the Rays, Ben Walker disappeared for two days. On Tuesday morning while at the Ray home, he complained of chlorea morbeus (gastroenteritis), left the room and was not seen again until Thursday when he appeared in Louisville and arranged for a preliminary hearing for McElroy on the following Monday.

The hearing was delayed till Tuesday as a second suspect, Hewlett or (Hulett) Ray, was arrested upon an affidavit of Elbert Vowell, the man that was providing housing for Walker.

This hearing was not held before Judge McLean but before Justice McAlilly. There is no record of this hearing or of the affidavit. There is no record of any evidence that Walker may have submitted against McElroy and Ray.

The state asked for a continuance until the next day stating that four key witnesses were not present. Those witnesses were not named and they never appeared.

On the following day, the County Attorney, J. B. Gully quickly asked that all charges be dropped and stated that there was no evidence that these two men were involved in Janie Sharp's murder.

McElroy & Ray were released and almost immediately, Ben Walker was arrested and charged with attempting to bribe witnesses. Some claimed that he was charged with perjury as well. Walker claimed that his witnesses were intimidated and afraid to testify but never alluded to any specific witnesses or evidence.

Throughout the proceeding, Will Sharp sat beside McElroy and publicly proclaimed his innocence.

As quoted in the Star Herald – a special to the Commercial Appeal, Sharp said, *"I believe in his entire innocence. He knows no more about the murder of my poor child than a stranger. Ray (Hewlett) is innocent also. It's a crying shame the way they are arresting innocent people. It's merely a subterfuge to create sympathy for the crime. I*

*am going to see them through, for they are as
innocent as a newborn babe."*

As a result of these charges, Walker's already
questionable reputation was further damaged and it
certainly increased animosity toward him and his
actions.

The local newspaper, The Winston County Journal,
attempted to interview him after the hearing and
made no attempt to hide its contempt for Walker's
actions in the case, calling for him to be dealt with
harshly if the charges proved to be true.

The story made newsprint as far away as Mobile,
Alabama and the Boston Evening Transcript. These
articles stated that a mob had gathered with a
desire to storm the Winston County jail and lynch
Walker for his actions. This was, without doubt, an
exaggeration.

No records indicate if these bribery charges were
pursued or later dropped.

Walker remained in the area throughout the winter
and it was assumed that he continued to work on
the case, although he may have pursued other
activities as well. While in the area, he continued to
stay in the home of Elbert Vowell. (who had filed
the affidavit against Hewlett Ray).

On the spring evening of March 20, 1912, Ben
Walker was at home with Elbert Vowell. The hour

was not late but darkness had fallen and the two men were sitting together quietly. Walker was reading by the light of a lamp near a window.

The stillness of that rural homestead was suddenly shattered by a shotgun blast and the sound of breaking glass. Vowell reached for his gun as he saw Walker fall to the floor amongst the broken glass and blood. He ran outside in the darkness and fired at what he believed to be two men riding away on horseback. At some distance, the men returned fire before disappearing into the night.

Elbert Vowell returned to his home and found Detective Ben Walker in a heap on the floor. The shooter had been close- Walker was nearly decapitated by the blast of buckshot.

The current sheriff was in the state capital on business and the murder was investigated by a Deputy Sheriff Clark and the now ex-sheriff Hull *(who was now the Winston County Circuit Clerk)*. They quickly arrived at the scene but found no clues of significance and the investigation went nowhere.

Of course, speculations were rampant:

Had someone in the Sharp family or close to the Sharp family had enough of Walker's meddling and attempts to find another suspect and decided to put an end to it?

Had Janie's real killer(s) believed that Walker was close to finding the truth or even had information to prove their guilt and chose to silence him?

Or perhaps Walker's death was not related at all to Janie's murder and his other activities had been the cause of his murder.

There are no details of any investigation into his death. No one else was wounded and no suspects were ever named in the death of Detective Ben Walker. His body was not claimed by any family members and his involvement in the Janie Sharp case is the only record of his existence.

A search of records in Cleveland and Bolivar County revealed no one of the age or race who could be identified as the detective. The common nature of his surname and the confusion of the names Ben, Hugh or Dan makes further identification almost impossible.

Ben Walker was buried on March 22, 1912 in the small rural Wood Cemetery next to the Small Wood Church located on a knoll in southwest Winston County. It is not known for certain but it is probable that the Elbert Vowell family made the arrangements for his burial. Walker's grave is located in the northeast area of the cemetery and is slightly offset from the surrounding row of graves.

Again, it is uncertain but it is likely that his grave was unmarked for many years. Currently there is a simple headstone that appears to have been placed there in the last thirty to forty years. It simply reads: *Ben Walker Died Mar 21, 1912.*

Many of the surrounding graves are those of the Vowell family. It is interesting to note that there are a few grave markers with the McElroy name scattered in the cemetery.

Ben Walker's marker in Small Wood Cemetery

CHAPTER 8
Walter Permenter

The second trial of Swinton Permenter for the murder of Janie Sharp had been delayed until the late summer of 1912. In the interest of providing Permenter with a fair trial with an impartial jury and concerns about possible violence after the verdict, the venue had been moved from Louisville to Winona in Montgomery County.

In that two-year period, life went on as usual for Winston Countians that were not directly involved in the case. Families raised their crops and their children and attended to their daily lives.

The upcoming trial was pushed from the headlines by national and world events. To put the changing times into perspective, a few of those events are chronicled here:

1911:

The first Indianapolis 500 took place; won by Ray Harroun in the "Marmon Wasp."

The Supreme Court rules that the Standard Oil Company constituted an unreasonable monopoly under the Sherman Antitrust Act.

Machu Picchu, "the Lost City of the Incas" was discovered in the mountains of Peru by American historian Hiram Bingham.

The first transcontinental flight across the United States was completed over a period of nearly three months.

1912:

New Mexico and Arizona were admitted to the union as the 47th and 48th states.

The race to the South Pole concluded as the Norwegian, Roald Amundsen reached the Pole ahead of Royal Navy officer Robert Falcon Scott.

One of the largest volcanic eruptions of the Twentieth Century took place in Alaska.

The Bull Moose Party holds its first convention.

These times also saw the birth of historic figures and organizations:

Ronald Reagan, Hubert Humphrey, Ginger Rogers, Danny Kaye, Roy Rogers, Tennessee Williams, Robert Johnson, Lucille Ball, Mahalia Jackson, Jack Ruby and Josef Mengele were born in 1911.The Chevrolet car company and IBM were established in 1911 as well as the formation of the Boy Scouts.

Danny Thomas, Tip O'Neill, Eva Braun, Milton Friedman, Minnie Pearl, Sonny Boy Williamson, Julia Child, Jackson Pollock, Woodie Guthrie, Ben Hogan and Jay Silverheels were born in 1912. Paramount and Universal Pictures as well as L.L. Bean were founded in 1912.

The sinking of the Titanic grabbed world headlines in April, 1912. News reports in Mississippi came from the wire services but there was a Mississippi connection. After some confusion, it was determined that a Mississippi man, A.N. Lahaud, was one of the victims.

Lahaud was a Biloxi resident with Syrian roots. Reports were that he had been visiting his childhood home and had intended to leave Europe to return to Mississippi around the same time that the *Titanic* sailed for the United States.

When lists of survivors and victims began appearing after the wreck, an individual named Sekas Lahoud appeared on listings of the victims. Lahaud's parents, also residents of Biloxi, were not sure that this was their son but it was later confirmed by a family member that Lahaud had indeed been aboard. His body was never recovered.

In a tragedy closer to home, a train carrying Confederate veterans from Texas to a reunion in Macon, Georgia derailed on the New Orleans and Northeastern railroad near Hattiesburg, Mississippi in May. There were as many as fifteen victims including four railroad employees, the engineer and fireman, two women and two small children.

*****

Despite these events and the cares of everyday life, the trial was still present in the minds of Winston County residents. Rumors continued that Swinton's older brother, Walter, had information gathered by the now murdered Ben Walker that was instrumental in the case.

Edward Walter Permenter was 12 years older than his brother but of similar build and appearance. The oldest surviving son of the Permenter family (an older brother died at the age of two) Walter was his brother's staunchest defender and took the lead role in the family's involvement with the case.

By all indications, Walter Permenter (known by his family as Walton) was a good man – a young man trying to build a better life for his family. Just thirty at the time of Janie's murder, Walton's family was growing with the birth of a second child earlier in the spring of 1910.

Walter (Walton) Permenter

Living on his father's farm in Rural Hill, Walton took a job in Louisville to supplement the family income. Working for W. J. Tabor, a prominent merchant in town, Walton probably performed several functions.

Writings indicate that Walton had a better education than some and he appeared to have a good head for figures. He certainly had a good reputation with Tabor and it was reported that Tabor had financed some of the defense of his brother, Swinton.

Walton was active in the defense of his brother and may have had a working relationship with the detective, Ben Walker. Walton made efforts at his own investigations but was surely limited by time and probable lack of cooperation from many in the community.

Walton kept a Crown Pocket notebook in the days after Janie's murder. It was not well organized nor did it contain any information as to specific suspects or direct evidence. It was a hodgepodge of information including lists of alibi witnesses, statements made by individuals for and against Swinton, statements made about the tracking dog and its handling, comments heard outside of the first grand jury hearing and measurements from the murder scene to various locations and homes in the community. There was no direct reference to the detective Ben Walker or any attempt at collaboration.

Although the pages were not dated, it became apparent that after the first few months, Walton's notes become less frequent and more sporadic and there was little or no reference to the upcoming second trial.

It is obvious that the notebook was used by family members after Walton's death for such mundane things as grocery and shopping lists and lists of accounts. Some entries were as late as 1926, fourteen years after Walton's death.

Like most people who took notes for personal use, Walton's handwriting was hurried. Comments recorded were not always referenced to a particular individual, sometimes lists of names were recorded but without any explanation. Over the years, the penciled text has faded, making some sections difficult if not impossible to read.

Below are a few but not all examples of the entries in the notebook. Words that are unclear are indicated by asterisks:

***

Threts (probably threats)

Tom McCool told **** that if Tabor came to Rural Hill and talked, They would <u>put him out.</u>

Tom McCool told Robert and Luther Horne, If Walker took sides on stand with the Permenter side too much they would put him out from there.

***

Hulit _ Salen?

Told Ben Van (landingham) that they had discovered tracks in only two places in the little branch and in the old trail that leads through Commel? Ray's ~~cotton~~ field.

Hulit said that there was a woman's track and two men tracks with it and he would be willing to swear to it being her track.

***

~~Jerry Black~~ Hammer? Said there were two in it. That the dog wanted to go farther.

Forrest Ray came out of Grand Jury room and talked with Hulit and Hulit came out and they both ***** Earl to one side and talked with him before he went in the room.

George Clark said he saw something done with the clothes which he would have to tell.

***

Lawrence Black said Swinton was in the search when he came about nine oclock.

Skeen? Said the dog was not reliable. I have been out with it every time it has been out.

Ask Emmet Carr if he said he was afraid they made a mistake in letting the dog go down to Permenters

***

Will Gladney (top of page)

Mr Sharp said the girl left home immediately after early dinner to go to Rural Hill and right back.

She was gone so long her mother grew uneasy about her and went to look for her.

He heard someone say that night that they tracked the girl to the sand bed ***** in Rays field ***?

Hulit said if suspicions get any stronger he would shoot the **** out of him.

This in the first part of the night at church?????

***

George Clark said he liked to have seen a trick worked– which he would not have seen for $1000 – for he would be bound to tell it.

Lee Ray said he heard Swinton say that night in the search – not there? It no use to look in thiose woods next to Mr Sharps – he didn't think.

Ray was looking there when girl was found

***

Cleveland Shumaker (top of page)

Lee Sharp told ***(Me - page is damaged) *to just say it was three oclock when the boys left Burchfields.*

He told me that I could be excused from the Grand Jury as far as he was concerned. We don't want the defense to go.

Mrs Burchfield went to his home and mentioned that Swinton hindered her boys so much. Cleveland said his father would not let boys come and hinder them. He orderd Jesse **** (maybe Watts) *to leave once.*

***

That he waited after they looked at the clock till Alonzo watered, curried and groomed? His horse. They went ½ mile together

That the tracks were crossed by the searching parties – even between trail and road

That the dog wanted to continue the chase

No witness with the dog until in the road except owner and C. B. Ray

***

Brantly? Never mentioned? (Probably a reference to an attorney in the case) *That he was plowing when Nellie reach home 4:15 – she saw him different times that evening while potting? Flowers.*

That Mrs Ball gave the Ray girls handkerchief also that Estell Ray was at Indian Springs and in Walton Permenter's buggy

That Dr. Blanton testified that she was structed" on the head with something sharp or at least a square (or sharp) corner, not a pistol

***

Squire McAlilly ask Dr. Blanton if the girl had been ravished before, after or about, the she was murdered. ***** *She undoubtedly has been.*

The girl came to her death at the hands of a man who wore a 9 or 91/2 shoe.

***

Walton had several notes related to distances from the murder scene and other locations around the community. The following is an example:

From Rural Hill to Rays by public road 2537 yds

"path 2518

From Rural Hill to place of capture 918

" to her home 740

Sharp to Rays 1654

Burchfields to permenters 1765

Burchfield to stump 2370

" to head of hollow 2600?

*Stump to **** 1950*

*Hollow to **** 1720*

Place of capture to murder   1440

From murder to lowest struggle 198 yd

Murder to road 182

Permenter to head of hollow   335?

The notebook along with several other pieces of information surfaced after the publication of "Murder in Rural Hill" in 2016. While it shed some light on the event and inconsistencies of the case against Swinton, there was no smoking gun and no direct accusations against others.

****

As the August trial approached, Swinton spent the days prior at the home of a family member in Eupora, Mississippi. Whether he had spent considerable time here is unknown but is a strong possibility due to the hostile environment around Rural Hill and McCool.

Eugene Shewmate was said to be a brother-in-law to Swinton and Walter. There was some confusion in newspaper reports that the name was Shumaker or Shumacher but the general consensus of opinion was that Shewmate was the correct name.

Walter intended to join Swinton in Eupora prior to the trial scheduled for August 5th. Walter's wife, Maddie and his children were residing with family in Preston, Mississippi (probably to shelter them from the trial and the bad blood in Rural Hill).

On Thursday, August 1st, Walter wrote a letter to Madie. He was apparently staying in Louisville where he worked and planned to head to Eupora the next day. The following is the content of that letter:

Louisville, Miss 8-1-12

Dear Madie: I wonder how you and babies are now. I have just finished dinner and as my pen and paper is handy, I thought I would write you a few lines. Have just finished the cake you left. It kept nice, did not get hard at all. I stayed here last night. I am very busy as this is the first and Bills to make and collect. But I would rather be busy now.

I will carry our chicklings to Mrs. Lewis tonight, haven't made any arrangements for Pigy yet.

I had the Journal send to you at Preston for 3 weeks beginning with this copy. I thought it you would like it.

*May remember Boon Duff who killed Lollar and was tried the second time this court. ***

He was brought here yesterday by his brother and turned over to the sheriff. His brother and mother came off of his bond so he will have to lie in jail. I geus guess from what I hear he is a terrible bad man, his people have spent a lot of money on him. The paper I guess will have the particulars.

Madie, Enoch Tollison owes us $6.68 for lumber. I told Eliza to tell him to send it to me by Mr. Hinze. but I don't look for it. I thought I would tell you so you would know. If it should be necessary you can write Mr. Hinze to collect it for you. Just clip out this if you like or write him yourself better. There will be 10% Interest if he does not send it now.

I saw Lucy this morning, she wants to know how you and babies were. You got a letter from Miss Esther – I had to break it, I thought maybe you would pardon me as I was curious to know what she had to say.

Love and kisses, - Your only one Walton

*(As best that can be determined, Boone Duff was an outlaw from the Pontotoc area who was imprisoned in Louisville awaiting trial or arraignment. It is likely that this was a change of venue much like Swinton's case. It is apparent that the Circuit court was in session in Louisville prior to its upcoming session in Winona.)

On Friday, August 2nd, while traveling to Eupora, Walter sent postcards to not only Madie but also to his children, Esther and Irwin. These along with the above letter were postmarked at 5:00 pm in the little town of Mathiston:

Dear Madie

I arrived here OK. Hope you are well. I guess I will stop to see Annie. I will write soon. Walton

Dear Little Esther

Papa is a way off down here and how he does wish to see his darling little Babe. Be good and don't cry. Papa is coming home soon.

Lovingly, Papa

Dear little Irwin

Hope you are well and playing with Dogie. Papa would like to see you so much this morning. Be good and don't bother mama.

Much love, Papa

Walton Permenter's postcard to his daughter on the day of his death.

Walter arrived in Eupora without incident. The brothers intended to leave the Shewmake home on the next day, Saturday, and arrive at Winona where the trial was to begin on the following Monday.

The following information came from several sources but the Progress Warden issue of August 8, 1912 (Eupora, Ms.) provided the most detail.

Around nine o'clock on that Friday evening, Swinton retired for the night. A short while later around ten o'clock, Walter took a bucket outside to the back porch for some water. Eugene Shewmake had just returned inside the home after emptying a waste bucket. As Walter was drawing the water, he was struck by a shotgun blast.

He was hit in the head, neck and chest by the blast and fell off the porch. Reports are that he died within a few moments. Shewmake doused all the lights in the home fearing more shots from the assailant.

The sound of the shotgun blast roused the neighborhood and people quickly appeared and rushed to the scene. No one had seen anything - except for one young man, Noel Myers, who claimed to see a single individual running away from the Shewmake house across a vacant lot near Adams Avenue, just moments after the shot was fired. The night passed without further incident but there no clues as to the identity or the whereabouts of the murderer.

The next day, a bloodhound procured from the Sheriff in Aberdeen was brought to the scene at around eight in the morning and they soon picked up a trail that led southward from the home and around a cotton house at the Eupora Gin Company. The trail continued further toward Winston County and into the Big Black Swamp located just south of the town of Eupora. The dogs eventually lost the trail in the hills and rugged swampland.

The next day, a young boy stumbled upon a shotgun hidden in the cotton house; The weapon was concealed in a tow sack and placed under a pile of bagging scraps.

Local newspaper reports indicated that it was an older breach loading weapon with one spent shell in the chamber and an additional shell containing buckshot. Several more shells were found outside of the cotton house.

The newspaper indicated that the weapon had some unique markings that might help in identifying the owner. It was turned over to the city marshal in Eupora.

Uncertain as to the status of Walton's family, his body was almost immediately embalmed and prepared for burial on Saturday.

*****

On Sunday, Ed Permenter, Elbert Vowell and his two sons and possibly W. J. Tabor made the trip to Eupora to return the body to Winston County. They openly discussed the case with friends and the local newspaper.

More intrigue was added to the incident when the Permenters indicated that a man from the Rural Hill area had been missing from that community for most of the previous week and suggested that he might be involved. This man was never identified and there was apparently no further investigation.

Due to the circumstances, there was debate as to where Walter should be interred. The original plans were for internment in Hopewell Cemetery located in Choctaw County with other family members but by the time the party arrived back in Winston County, the decision was made for burial in the Masonic Cemetery within the City of Louisville. No reason was indicated for that decision, but it is probable that concerns for the safety of the family and the condition of the body were the primary considerations.

Edward Walter Permenter had not lived to see his 32nd birthday. He left a pregnant wife and two small children.

Again, there was a great deal of speculation by residents and the media. Some believed that in the darkness, Walter was mistaken for Swinton because of his comparable size and appearance. Others suspected that Walter was the intended victim because of the information that he held in the case, possibly gathered from Ben Walker prior to his death.

The only record of his death is from newspaper reports. There are no further records of the investigation in Eupora or Webster County. No one was ever charged in the case or even a suspect named. Just like Ben Walker, Walter Permenter became another forgotten victim of this tragic case.

Further newspaper reports indicated that the current governor of Mississippi, Earl L. Brewer offered a $500 reward for the capture of Walton Permenter's assassin as well as an additional reward for the assassin of Ben Walker.

It had been more than two years since Janie Sharp's murder. Cases had been prepared, arrangements had been made and the trial would not be delayed for long.

Due to two previous continuances, after only a one-week delay, the final trial of Ernest Swinton Permenter would take place on August 12, 1912.

CHAPTER 9.
The Trial Begins

George Alonzo McLean fit the stereotype as a Southern circuit riding judge of the early 20th century. Born in 1859 to a genteel slaveholding family, George slept with a companion slave boy at the foot of his bed until the end of the Civil War.

McLean studied law and served a term in the Mississippi Senate before settling into life as a circuit judge in the 5th District of Mississippi. This District encompassed six counties including Winston. His duties required holding court sessions twice a year in each county.

He had four children with his first wife who died from complications giving birth at a young age. A few years later he remarried and had two additional children.

The youngest child was George Alonzo McLean, Jr. who achieved success as the owner/publisher of The Tupelo Daily Journal and a community activist. The younger McLean is the subject of the book: *Tupelo Man – the Life and Times of George McLean, a Most Peculiar Newspaper Publisher by Robert Blade*. Much of the information concerning Judge McLean was derived from this book.

The McLean household in Winona was a boisterous one and the Judge was not involved in the day-to-day activities of his children until a situation dictated that a stern Presbyterian hand be applied.

McLean was a major landowner and controlled as much as ten thousand acres of farmland at one time. He was an early automobile enthusiast and drove a Model T to range about the countryside and inspect his properties. He once took the family on a trip across the West reaching as far as Pike's Peak in a Franklin Touring car.

The Judge was tall, lean, proper and well respected by his peers. The Supreme Court ruling that overturned the conviction in the first trial of Swinton Permenter was a bitter pill for him to swallow. He had every intention of conducting a procedurally proper and well-disciplined second trial. The publicity surrounding the case would demand it. The legal profession, every politician and every reporter in the state of Mississippi and many across the country had all eyes upon this proceeding.

The prosecution recognized the gravity of the case as well and the area District Attorney T. L. Lamb of Eupora was assisted by as many as six additional counsels, including the Montgomery County Attorney Wellborn, W.S. Knox of Winona, the former District Attorney Rueben Jones and his son, H.F. Jones of Louisville, J. A. Teat of Kosciusko and ex-Congressman Shed Hill. Hill took the lead on much of the questioning during the trial.

Not to be outdone, the defense gathered as many as six attorneys. Swinton Permenter's original legal team from the first trial consisting of H.H. Rodgers, L.H. Hopkins and Z.A. Brantley was still intact. Local attorneys, Witty and Thompson were added as a late addition and the lead attorney was a well-known barrister from Hazelhurst named R.N. Miller. After the trial began, a former district attorney from the 6th District and now a practicing attorney in Memphis, J.B. Webb, joined the defense team.

*****

The small town of Winona in central Mississippi would be the center of attention of the entire state and much of the nation over the next 12 days as newspaper reporters and members of the legal profession crowded into the area. Winona was a well-established community nestled in the hills just to the east of the fertile Mississippi Delta.

Winona was significantly larger than Louisville at that time. The population of twenty-five hundred was fed by the intersection of two railroads and its proximity to the vast farmlands of the Delta.

Much like Natchez, another more famous city farther to the south, Winona benefitted when affluent landowners of Delta lands chose to live in the nearby hill communities believing that it was a healthier environment with fewer mosquitoes and diseases.

Winona continued to prosper despite a yellow fever epidemic that decimated the population in 1878 and a fire, ten years later, that destroyed the downtown business district.

***

In an interesting side note, Winona suffered through its own tragic and sensational murder case in 1996 when the owner and three employees of the downtown Tardy Furniture Company were brutally murdered. The case garnered national attention over a period of more than twenty years.

The murders took place just a short distance from the location of the old courthouse where Swinton Permenter was tried in 1912. Curtis Flowers, a young black man was arrested and tried months after the killings. Flowers had been fired from the store and prosecutors believed revenge was the motive.

The evidence was circumstantial at best. Prosecutors centered on Flowers to the exclusion of other suspects, much like the Rural Hill case. Over the next thirteen years, Flowers would be tried six times for the crimes. Convicted in the first three trials, all would be overturned at the state level for reasons including racial bias.

After two additional mistrials, Flowers was again convicted and sentenced to death in 2010. This time the Mississippi Supreme Court upheld the conviction. It took three years to prepare an appeal for the case and another six years for the U. S. Supreme Court to overturn the conviction of Flowers in 2019.

The Mississippi Attorney General has refused to pursue further prosecution and most now believe that Flowers was not involved with the murders. Just like the Janie Sharp case in 1910, no one has ever been brought to justice for the murders of Bertha Tardy, Derrick "BoBo" Stewart, Carmen Rigby and Robert Golden.

***

There is no longer an official transcript of Swinton Permenter's second trial. Too many years have passed and too many custodians of these documents have come and gone. But the sensational nature of this case piqued the interest of newspapers across the country. One paper, The Commercial Appeal in Memphis, took a special interest and covered the case from beginning to end with special daily reports from the courtroom. These newspaper reports provided details of testimony and conflicts throughout the trial and are the basis for the following chapters.

The trial opened on Monday, August 12, 1912 in the courtroom of the Montgomery County Courthouse. The heat was oppressive as to be expected in Mississippi in August but it had no impact on the size of the crowd that had gathered to watch this legal battle. The courtroom and gallery were packed and there were even a few ladies in the audience, which was extremely rare in rural Mississippi in the early 1900's.

Regardless of the heat and the size of the crowd, good order was maintained throughout the trial. The only real interruption in the proceedings occurred when Judge McLean ordered bailiffs to find and install electric fans to cool witnesses and sometimes members of the audience.

Judge McLean opened court proceedings at 2:00 pm, the hottest time of the day. After each side announced their readiness to continue, jury selection began. One hundred possible jurors had received summons and were on hand to be questioned by the prosecution and defense teams.

Men were brought to the jury box in groups of twelve– this man eliminated for this bias, another eliminated for a connection to someone associated with the case, yet another not considered for some perceived prejudice. It was 7:00 pm when the court was adjourned for the night. Only six jurors had been selected out of the first fifty interviewed.

Taking extra caution, Judge McLean had arranged for four special bailiffs to assist with the case and to care for and monitor the jurors. The six jurors selected to this point were instructed demonstratively to not discuss the case among themselves in any form and the bailiffs were instructed to not allow anyone to approach them.

Jury selection began again on Tuesday morning and it took until the noon break to seat a full jury of twelve men. These men were of Montgomery County and had no known connections to the case or the families involved. Interestingly enough, all were listed as farmers.

According to the Commercial Appeal, they ranged from the age of 24 to 45 and most were family men.The jury is listed as follows:

J.R. Bennett, J.F. Castles, M.H. Ferguson, G.C. Ingram, W.D Loweriman, J.T. Mann, T. H. Moose, Fred Parker, E.M. Stephens, L. H. Sykes, J.G Taylor and J.W. Tinnon

Testimony would begin after lunch at 1:00 pm and if it was possible, the courtroom was more crowded than on Monday. According to the Commercial Appeal – "a surging crowd of humanity filled every available space in the courtroom, and so oppressive did it become that

*Judge McLean dispatched bailiffs for fans for the
jury, attorneys and some of the spectators."*

*This marker is all that remains of the Montgomery
County Courthouse from 1912.*

CHAPTER 10
The Prosecution's Case

Trial testimony comes almost exclusively from a series of Commercial Appeal articles. Subject to space limitations, the interpretations of the reporter and the complex and sometimes conflicting testimony, the reader may find the following chapters confusing and contradictory at times.

TUESDAY, AUGUST 13, 1912

Testimony began after the lunch break as the prosecution began its case. Martha E. Sharp, the mother of Janie Sharp, was the first to testify. Mrs. Sharp was dressed in black from head to toe to convey that she was still in mourning for her daughter. She was composed throughout her testimony. The District Attorney began by asking Mrs. Sharp to relay the incidents of the day of the murder.

Martha Sharp testified that Miss Janie had helped her clean away the dishes from the noon meal and had decided to take the one and a half mile walk from their home to the post office and stores in Rural Hill. She intended to pick up the family's mail and make some purchases of sewing needs.

The handkerchief found in Swinton Permenter's pocket was admitted into evidence. Mrs. Sharp was asked to identify it. She was at first uncertain until Prosecutor Teal provided his glasses for her use. Upon donning the spectacles, she identified it as Janie's, noting a small tear in one corner of the cloth.

Mrs. Sharp continued her testimony, indicating that she became concerned when Janie did not return home by late in the day and went in search of her daughter. Mrs. Sharp indicated that the girl would have traveled along the Commodore Road and that there were no houses directly on the road for her to pass. To her knowledge, Janie had not been seen along the road.

In cross examination, defense attorney Miller attempted to question Mrs. Sharp's identification of the handkerchief. She was unwavering in her certainty, stating that it was the same one that Janie had on the day of the murder. When asked how she could be certain, she indicated that it was a prized gift from Janie's grandmother and had been given to her about a year before her death.

Miller continued to aggressively question Mrs. Sharp about the handkerchief until Judge McLean intervened and instructed the defense to move on.

When asked about the Permenter family, Mrs. Sharp noted that they were neighbors and had been on good terms prior to the murder. She was adamant that there was no courting relationship between Swinton and her daughter, Janie.

After Mrs. Sharp's testimony, the prosecution presented a number of witnesses who had seen Janie that day with the goal of establishing a timeline of events.

Oscar McWhorter testified that he was at Rural Hill that afternoon and had seen Janie. He had left his home around noon and traveled to Rural Hill that day with a wagon to be loaded with an engine. He stated that he was standing by his loaded wagon when Janie came out of Williams' store. He noted that she had a parasol and some bundles in her hand as she left. He indicated that he was somewhat certain of the time as he heard the store clock strike three as he pulled away from Rural Hill.

In cross examination, Defense Attorney Miller questioned the legitimacy of McWhorter's testimony and asked if he had previously read his testimony over from the first trial in Winston County. McWhorter admitted that someone had read it to him from the record as he wanted to refresh his memory.

The next witness was Yancey Lowery. Lowery's wife was a cousin of Swinton Permenter. He was also in Rural Hill that afternoon and had seen Janie at the store. He remained at the store after Janie left and believed that the store clock struck three about fifteen or twenty minutes after Janie left.

Under cross examination, Lowery was asked if he had seen a handkerchief in Janie's hand while at the store. He indicated that he had but could not identify it or determine if it had been freshly laundered.

The store owner, Dill (later referred to as Josh) Williams was the next to testify. He recalled that Janie had been at the store sometime after dinner (in the South, the noon day meal is often referred to as dinner) but he could not say the exact time.

He did remember selling yarn and spool thread and wrapping them in separate packages for Janie. He did not have the trimmings that Janie was looking for and she left to go to the other store in Rural Hill, Shumach's. She did not find the items there and returned to his store before she left Rural Hill. He also stated that she indicated that she would be going to the Cyrus Ray home when she left Rural Hill.

Three other witnesses testified that they had also seen Janie that day. Van Schemata said he was near the store and saw Janie leave about the time that the store clock struck three. Miss Lois Schumacher also claimed to see Janie that day with her bundles and parasol.

Bessie Ray was the last witness of the day. She was not specifically identified but investigation reveals that she was a young woman of approximately the same age as Janie and Swinton Permenter and likely a cousin of Janie's. Her testimony was limited to the handkerchief. When handed to her, she positively identified it as the one belonging to Janie.

A reasonable timeline had been established. Janie had left Rural Hill and proceeded to Commodore Road, likely to the home of Cyrus Ray between 2:45 pm and 3:20 pm.

As the first day of testimony closed, it became apparent that much of the case would hinge upon the handkerchief found in Swinton's possession. If the jury believed it to be Janie's without a reasonable doubt, it would be difficult for the defense team to provide a plausible explanation.

WEDNESDAY, AUGUST 14, 1912

Court resumed at 8:30 am with more witnesses concerning Janie's presence at Rural Hill and the time frame.

John Holden indicated that he was at Rural Hill at the time of the mail delivery – around 1:00 pm and remained there for a period of time. He did not recall seeing Janie. Under cross examination, he noted that he spent time at Shumach's store and did not see her there or at the William's store during that time.

Claude Massey was the next to testify. His recollection was that he actually met Janie on the Commodore Road about a quarter mile from Rural Hill after she left. Defense Attorney Rogers asked if Massey had seen anyone else on the road that afternoon. He denied seeing anyone.

Rogers then created a stir in the courtroom when he asked, "Didn't you tell Church Edwards at the Hinze Post Office that you saw Hewlett Ray and Tom McElroy on the Commodore Road that evening?

Massey replied, "No sir, I did not!"

After Massey left the stand, a map was submitted into evidence. The sheriff at the time of the murder, J.W. Gully, had made a map of the Commodore Road and the paths traveled by Janie on the day of the murder. This was submitted for the jury to examine.

It had been assumed that over the years, the map had been lost or destroyed. In my research and conversations, there was little interest or further reference to this map. One can imagine my surprise and excitement, when this very map was found not only to still exist but to be in excellent condition and made available for me to review.

In an act that would certainly not be possible today, the map was given to the Permenter family after the trial and has been held in safekeeping for more than one hundred years. On the following page is a section of the map indicating the area around the murder scene.

The next witness called would spend five hours on the stand. Lee Sharp was Janie's older brother and was convinced of Swinton Permenter's guilt from the beginning as his testimony would indicate.

His testimony began as he spoke of the search for his sister on Thursday evening, July 21, 1910. He stated that he and a group of men from the community were searching along Commodore Road and entered a strip of woods on the east side of the road. It was here that they saw Swinton for the first time that evening around 10:00 pm.

Lee stated that Swinton was alone and on foot and upon approaching the party of men, he lay down by a small tree. Lee told Permenter that Janie had disappeared and they were out looking for her and feared the worst.

A section of the map used in the 1912 trial of Swinton Permenter

Permenter stated that he did not know where she was but "a nigger might have done it." Lee indicated that he saw a pistol in Permenter's pocket at that time.

The men continued to search; some wanted to search farther north but Lee suggested that they go further east. They came upon some thick brush and prepared to search it when Permenter said, "Boys' it's no use going in there. I've hunted those woods thoroughly." Lee wanted to search in the underbrush but for some reason did not at that time.

Sharp stated that as the moon had gone down, some men lit torches and continued the search over a large area of fields and woods. Permenter stayed with them throughout the search. As the party reached an area northwest of Rural Hill, Lee stated that Permenter made a strange statement.

"Let's go look on yonder way" pointing in a direction opposite of where Janie's body was eventually found. Putting his hand over his breast, Permenter then said, "Something in here tells me she's back that way."

Sharp indicated that they continued to search until the early morning hours before deciding to break for daylight.

He returned to the area prior to everyone else at around 6:00 am. Lee began his search not far from the Sharp home as he scanned the west side of the Commodore Road. *(there may be some missing content here relative to the road reference or his actions or Lee may have mis-spoke as Janie's body was actually located on the east side of Commodore Road. There was a path or minor road leading in a southeasterly direction from the Commodore Road and the body was found on the southwest side of this path. This may be the cause of confusion.)* He entered a small ravine that led to a branch. It was here that he found the body of his sister.

Lee Sharp said that Janie's body was lying flat in the branch partially submerged in the water with one leg sticking out. He saw that her throat had been cut halfway around and there was a "powerful bruise" on her head as if done by a pistol butt. Between her legs lay her parasol and on her left side lay the bundles from the store. Sharp testified that he did not move her body and that he shrieked several times for help.

Sharp also indicated that after Janie's funeral on Saturday, he returned to the scene and began searching for clues. He observed tracks coming from the Commodore Road that appeared to be those of a man and woman and a spot where it appeared that a scuffle took place. The tracks continued and the signs of another scuffle were observed. Sharp noted that the tracks were far apart as if the parties were running. He also indicated that these tracks were about two hundred yards from the Sharp home.

The prosecution now directed questioning towards Permenter's behavior and dress at the time of the murder.

Sharp indicated that as Janie's body was moved to the Sharp home, Permenter was heard to say, "Well, I'll have to go home and change my clothes. Would have been here last night but I was feeling bad."

When asked what clothes Swinton Permenter was wearing on the night of the search, Lee indicated a suit of blue serge and that he had that same suit on the next morning.

At this time, the court broke for lunch till 2:00 pm when Sharp resumed his testimony. The courtroom continued to be packed as the crowd suffered through the heat, not wanting to miss a single word of the trial.

The prosecution opened in the afternoon by submitting a pair of shoes belonging to the suspect. These shoes were described as low quarter shoes. *(Low quarter shoes are shoes where the upper does not extend above the bony projection of the ankle)* One of the shoes submitted had a hole in the sole. Sharp identified them as the shoes worn by Permenter on the night of the search.

At this point, the defense submitted a second pair of high quarter shoes as the ones worn by Permenter.

Based upon the question of the shoes, the ex-sheriff, A. P. Hull was called as a witness for the prosecution but his testimony relative to the shoes was not helpful. He identified the high quarter shoes as the ones he received from his deputy along with clothing belonging to the defendant. He noted that they were wet when he received them. He also identified the handkerchief as the one provided to him by the deputy.

W. R. Hull, the former deputy who collected the clothes from the Permenter home, identified the clothing and shoes and indicated that he had taken them to the jail in Winona and Permenter had identified them as his property.

The witch-hazel stick that had been cut at the scene of the crime to measure the footprints was then submitted into evidence. When compared to the high quarter shoes, the stick did not match the shoe size.

Before the conclusion of that day's proceedings, testimony was provided by Cyrus Ray. Little is known about this and was not directly referred to in newspaper reports. It seemed to have no direct bearing on the case.

Lee Sharp specifically identified Swinton Permenter's shoes as those that he wore on the night of the search for Janie. From a reasonable perspective, it would seem unlikely that a distraught man would even be aware of another man's shoes at that time much less be able to positively identify them.

Countered with the deputy's testimony that the shoes he collected from Permenter the next day were wet as if they had been worn during the night, it would tend to negate the accuracy of Lee Sharp's testimony. Then given that the stick cut at the scene to measure the footprint did not match the shoe collected by the deputy, it would seem to discredit the shoe print evidence.

CHAPTER 11.
Suspicious Behavior

THURSDAY, AUGUST 15, 1912

As the trial resumed, Mrs. Permenter, the mother of Swinton, sat by his side for the first time. She was dressed in traditional black much like Mrs. Sharp on the first day of testimony although Mrs. Permenter had a more recent cause for her mourning due to the murder of her oldest son, Walter, just prior to the trial.

As if to counter the impact of Permenter's mother at his side, Janie's father, W. C. Sharp was in the courtroom for the first time since the trial started. According to reports, Mr. Sharp's physical condition had greatly deteriorated and was most likely affected by the strain and stress of having to deal with the murder of his daughter, the uncertainty of the trial and the drama of the past two years.

The courtroom was again packed with a full gallery and the heat was oppressive. The day's first witness was a young man named Forrest Ray. He was initially questioned by Prosecution Attorney Treat.

He testified that on the day of the murder, he had been at his home which was on the Sharp family's place. Later that day he went to the home of his uncle, Benton Ray, and there he saw Earl Ray and his sister, Nessie. Later, on that day between 4 and 5 o'clock, he went to a field that was near the Commodore Road with a gentleman by the name of Nathan Sharp and from there he went to the home of another uncle, Cyrus Ray.

It was here that he heard Cyrus Ray's daughter say, "You all had better be hunting for Janie. I just learned a little while ago she's missing and can't be found."

Forrest Ray indicated that this was the first time he knew anything about Janie Sharp missing. He testified that he first went to the Sharp home and then started toward Rural Hill. Along the way, he met Janie's Father.

At Mr. Sharp's request, Forrest Ray had searched along the Commodore Road to see if he could find any of Janie's tracks. He indicated that he did observe some tracks of a woman. From there he went back toward his uncle's home (Cyrus Ray) and while in the woods he saw several more tracks. The sight of the woman's tracks concerned him and he went on to his uncle's house and got a horse and with others rode to the home of Ol' Permenter which was located a short distance to the east of Commodore Road.

Ol' was an uncle of Swinton and his home was nearly a mile from that of Cyrus Ray's. It was also the closest home to the location where Janie's body was found – located on a ridge, a distance of a quarter mile or less from the scene.

Forrest Ray asked Ol' if he had seen any sign of Miss Janie and he replied that he had not. At this point, Ray and the group of men with him went back to the Commodore Road.

When they got back to the road, they found that a crowd of people had begun to gather to discuss and help with the search for Janie. They tied their horses and began to search on foot.

Forrest Ray testified that he first saw Swinton Permenter on the night of the search at around 10 p.m. He did state that he had been to the Permenter's house earlier and that he had not found Swinton there. He indicated that later that night, Permenter was with the party of searchers that included Lee Sharp as he had previously testified.

Forrest Ray also corroborated Lee Sharp's testimony about Permenter's statements concerning his search of the patch of woods.

The next witness that day was a man by the name of Earl Ray (reported as the fiancée of Janie) who lived only a quarter of a mile from the Sharp place at that time. His testimony corroborated much of what Forrest Ray had said.

He indicated that he was at home with his sisters till about 5:00 p.m. on the day of the murder. He then went to a field near Commodore Road and from there to his Uncle Cyrus Ray's home. Just like the previous witness, he testified that this was where he learned that Janie was missing.

From there he went to the Commodore Road to join in the search. Shortly before sunset, Earl Ray along with a man by the name of Tom McCool went to Ed Permenter's home and asked if anyone had seen Janie. Swinton was not there at the time.

They went back to the Commodore Road and joined the crowd but later returned for a second time to the Permenter home about dark and asked the family if Swinton was there. They were again told that Swinton was not there. Earl Ray stated that he later saw Swinton sometime between 10 and 11 o'clock that night on the road but did not hear the remarks that others claimed were made by Swinton.

He noted that Swinton was present the next morning when Janie's body was found and that he acted somewhat strangely and sat about 15 to 20 feet away from the crowd and lay down there at a small tree.

When cross-examined by the defense, Earl Ray admitted that he had interest in Miss Janie prior to her death and that there was another young man named Whitmire who also had interest in her as well. He acknowledged that he had been the fiancée of Miss Janie and that they had been engaged for more than a year. He also said that he had been at the Sharp home on the Sunday before the murder on the following Thursday.

The next prosecution witness was Hewlett Ray, one of the men accused by Ben Walker. He testified that on the day of the murder he was working on the farm that he had rented from Tom McElroy.

Late in the afternoon when he learned that Jamie had disappeared, he left his work chopping cotton in the field and later that evening went to the Permenter home with William and Forrest Ray - arriving there around 9 p.m. but saw no one there.

They got with a search party and later saw Swinton Permenter on the Commodore Road. Hewlett Ray corroborated the testimony by Lee Sharp and others that Permenter seemed to discourage the party from searching certain parts of the woods.

Under cross-examination by the Defense Attorney Miller, Hewlett Ray was asked if he had been informed that the detective Ben Walker was out and about hunting for people who may have killed Janie Sharp. He claimed he had not been aware of that. Defense Attorney Miller said, "Didn't you tell Walker to let you and your business alone and if he did not you would make it interesting for him?"

"No sir, I did not say any such thing."

When accused by the defense, he positively denied using foul language and brandishing a pistol in the crowd that next morning when Miss Janie's body was found.

Tom McElroy was the next witness. This caused a stir in the courtroom crowd as McElroy along with Hewlett Ray had temporarily been "arrested" by Ben Walker in the case. In his testimony he stated that at the time of Janie's murder he was living about a mile and one half from the Sharp home.

On that day he was at home with his father-in-law and mother-in-law. He noted that he received information that Janie was missing about sundown and he immediately went toward the Sharp home and along the way he met a group of men who were hunting for her.

McElroy indicated that they were all on the Commodore Road between 8 and 9 o'clock and he noted that like the others, he saw Swinton Permenter in the crowd at around 10 p.m. He also said that the last time he has seen Janie before her death was about two weeks prior.

Defense attorneys took the opportunity to ask him what shoe size he wore and he indicated that he wore a size nine. Under cross-examination he also denied having heard Hewlett Ray say that if Janie was found, her throat would be cut.

When asked, he informed the court that he sold his farm the following September in 1910 and moved to Texas in an effort to try to provide better for his family and himself. Defense Counsel Miller then asked if an affidavit had been made out against him for the murder of Janie Sharp.

The prosecution counsel Hill objected but then withdrew his objection and McElroy was instructed to answer. He said yes, an affidavit had been made against him.

When the prosecution was able to redirect, McElroy was asked about the outcome of the affidavit. There was an objection by the defense but after some discussion, Judge McClain overruled the objection and the witness indicated that the affidavit had been dismissed without prosecution.

The testimony continued throughout a long day with a parade of witnesses.

The prosecution's next witness was Tom McCool. During his testimony he indicated that he had reached the vicinity of the murder as darkness approached and joined in the search.

At some point, he went to the Ed Permenter home to see if Swinton was there but did not find him. As he returned along Commodore Road, he met Swinton and his uncle, Ol' Permenter, about a half mile from his home sometime between 9:00 and 10:00 pm.

McCool said that he asked Permenter, "Why ain't you not assisting in the search for Janie?"

He stated that Swinton replied, "Well, wait until I go home and get a horse to ride and I'll go with you."

McCool responded, "There's no use getting a horse. I am walking and so can you."

McCool's testimony was that Swinton consented to join him but implied that it took some persuasion on his part. As they walked along the road, the men heard a dog bark in the nearby woods and McCool said to Permenter: "I'll bet that dog is barking where Miss Janie's body is lying."

McCool indicated that Permenter responded, "Oh, it ain't nothing but a dead possum and it ain't no use for us to go in there."

McCool believed that Janie's body was found the next morning about two hundred yards from where he first met Permenter on the road that night.

The next witness for the prosecution was a man named Davis Steed. Steed lived in nearby Attala County but near the Hinze Post Office located south of Rural Hill. His testimony centered around a previous statement made by Swinton Permenter.

Steed testified that on a Saturday evening about two weeks before the murder, he attended a prayer meeting at the Horn schoolhouse and happened to be sitting beside Swinton. They began whispering about some of the local girls and he remarked that two of the girls in attendance that night were about the prettiest girls he had ever seen in his life.

He indicated that Swinton responded by referring to Janie Sharp and said he would give ten dollars and be willing to spend ten years of his life in jail to receive the affection of Janie.

The defense counsel questioned Steed about the statement and asked if he had been paid (hired) to make such a statement. Steed answered by emphatically denying the accusation.

The next witness was Dr. W. M. Clemmons, the dentist who lived near Rural Hill not far from the Williams' store. Clemmons' testimony was straightforward.

Clemmons said that he remembered the day well and upon hearing of Miss Janie's disappearance through a personal message he went to aid in the search.

Not far from Rural Hill, he met a group of men and joined them. At some point he left the group and went in search of the local Methodist minister named T. L. Oaks. Clemmons thought that perhaps Janie had eloped and married some young man in the community. After searching, he was not able to find the clergyman.

He later went to the home of Ol' Permenter with

two other men in hopes of finding Swinton there and that he might have some information but was not successful.

The next morning, he heard shouting on the Commodore Road and went to the spot where Janie's body was found. A Justice of the Peace named McAlilly was on the scene and because of his medical background, McAlilly requested that Clemmons examine the body. Clemmons approached Janie's corpse along with two other men and determined that she was indeed deceased and he described the position of the body and the nature of her wounds.

In the last part of his testimony, Clemmons shook the defense when he stated that he had heard Swinton remark that if old man Sharp (Janie's father) didn't mind he would be sorry for it someday. Clemmons believed the remark was made because Will Sharp had forbidden Permenter from visiting his home.

The next prosecution witness seemed to catch the prosecution off guard when under cross examination, Will Gladney acknowledged that Hewlett Ray (another of the men "arrested" by Ben Walker) had carried a shotgun during the search for Janie and had cursed and swore when her body was found.

He also stated that Hewlett Ray remarked that if suspicions against Permenter got much stronger he would shoot his damn brains out. This was in direct conflict with Hewlett Ray's testimony given earlier in the day.

The final witness of the day was Newt McCool and his statements centered around the search for Swinton Permenter on the night of the search. His testimony corroborated earlier testimony as he was also sent to Ol' Permenter's home by Will Sharp to ask about Swinton but could not find him.

CHAPTER 12
Tracking

FRIDAY, AUGUST 16, 1912

Court reconvened on Friday at 8:30 am. The courtroom was full again and Swinton's mother still by his side as she sat stone faced throughout the testimony. Will Sharp, Janie's father, was also in the courtroom in spite of the fact that he had become ill during the previous day.

The prosecution's next witness was John Edwards. Edwards had been on the scene when Janie's body was found. His testimony indicated that Swinton Permenter was there as well and as talk circulated that bloodhounds would certainly be brought in to track the killer, he heard Swinton remark that if dogs were brought into the search, they would certainly track him as he had been in those woods the night before searching for Janie.

In an effort to discredit Edwards, the defense forced him to admit that he had been convicted of carrying a concealed weapon in the past but also stated that he had no bad feelings toward Swinton or his family.

Webster Schumacher also testified that he heard Permenter make the same remark. When asked by the defense if he thought that the comment may have been made in jest, Schumacher indicated that he did not think so.

The next witness, Josh McGee, also testified to the statement made by Permenter. The defense team asked McGee if Permenter looked or acted peculiar throughout this time but the witness said he did not really pay attention to that. It was noted in his testimony that it had been raining and that he had loaned his raincoat to cover Janie's body.

The next major witness was not present in the courtroom. The reason that Terrell Hall did not appear was not stated in the newspaper report but both sides agreed to have his written testimony read into the record. Prosecutor Teal read to the jury:

Hall was at the Will Sharp home at around 9:00 am on the morning that Janie's body had been brought there. He was in the company of Swinton Permenter and asked Swinton if he could borrow a coat. They left the Sharp home and walked to Permenter's home.

Hall testified that he did not go inside but stood by the front gate. A few minutes passed and he saw Swinton come out to the porch with a wash pan, enter a right-hand side room of the house where he washed and changed clothes. He noted that Permenter had on a blue colored suit at first but came out in a different set of clothing. Swinton and other members of his family went back to the Sharp home riding in a wagon while Hall and Swinton's father walked the short distance. Later Hall walked back to the Permenter home with Mr. Permenter.

His written statement indicated that later, he went into the side room where Swinton had bathed and changed and found the clothes he had been previously wearing. He stated that in the pants pocket was a Barlow knife, a plug of tobacco and two handkerchiefs – one belonging to a man and the other was obviously a lady's handkerchief. He indicated that the lady's handkerchief was smaller and had figures around the border.

It was never stated in the testimony why he felt the need to examine Swinton's clothing.

J. T. Hanna was the next to testify for the prosecution. Hanna was the owner and handler of the bloodhound used that day. Hanna testified that he had trained dogs all his life as had his father and grandfather before him. The dog was a registered bloodhound named Ruth Hindoo and while she was only fourteen months old, she had proven her ability to track.

Hanna started the dog at the branch where Janie's body was found. According to his testimony the dog ran north along the branch for forty yards where the dog struck a hole of water and scented on top of the water. The dog then went down the east side of the branch and he noticed what appeared to be scuffed places on the ground. The dog then tracked in a southeasterly direction and not much farther, he noticed tracks that appeared to be made by a man and a woman. A few feet further down the branch, he observed a mule track. Tracking further the dog struck a small ravine and followed it up to an old road where a man's track was seen. The dog crossed the road and entered a nearby crossroad where Hanna saw more tracks made by a man and a woman.

The dog then trailed south and headed for the Ed Permenter farm. When the dog reached the corner of the yard of the home, Hanna checked her at the gate.

Someone in the crowd said, "let her go!" He released the dog who then headed to the road in front of the home and scented several men standing there before returning toward the house. The dog trailed around the home lot and the stable and barn before returning to the gate. She then angled across a nearby field of cotton before returning once again to the gate in front of the home.

It was here that Ed Permenter, Swinton's father met him and said, "Hello, Hanna, you look natural."

Hanna replied, "Yes, but I do want a drink of water."

The dog began tracking again and scented a group of five men standing nearby. Swinton Permenter was standing in the center of this group. According to Hanna, the dog looked Swinton over, scented him and threw his head back.

Hanna testified that at this point he saw Walter Permenter, Swinton's older brother, on the steps of the porch with what appeared to be a gun in his hand. His testimony implied that he was concerned that Walter might want to kill him or his dog.

Cyrus Ray was recalled to the stand to corroborate Hanna's testimony concerning the tracks seen near where Janie was found.

The last witness called was a man named Rueben Hunt who was in the party trailing the bloodhound. He also described the route taken by the dog.

As 5:00 pm approached, the prosecution rested its case. While a great deal of evidence was presented, most if not all was circumstantial - the very problem that led to the previous trial decision being overturned.

The prosecution's case would hinge upon convincing the jury that the handkerchief was indeed the one that Janie possessed at the time of her murder and establishing that Swinton Permenter was the only individual with the desire, opportunity and motive to take her life.

The trial would continue on Saturday and now the defense would have the opportunity to present its witnesses, refute the prosecution's witnesses and cast a reasonable doubt upon the guilt of Swinton Permenter.

CHAPTER 13.
The Defense

SATURDAY, AUGUST 17, 1912

The trial resumed at 8:30 on Saturday morning. Before the defense began to present its case, defense attorney Miller made a motion to dismiss the case against his client. He asked that all evidence submitted by the prosecution be excluded and for the judge to instruct the jury to find Swinton Permenter not guilty. Judge McLean immediately overruled the motion and instructed the defense to proceed.

The defense plan was simple; to call into question the timeline of events and prove that Swinton did not have an opportunity to commit the crime, repudiate or at least provide contradictory evidence to that provided by prosecution witnesses and to provide an explanation for the lady's handkerchief found in Permenter's clothing.

The defense's first witness was Buster Burchfield who had been at Rural Hill on the day of Janie's murder. He testified that he spoke with Josh Williams, the owner of the store, on the following day about the time that Janie left his store at Rural Hill.

Josh Williams was recalled by the defense and
asked about the time. Williams now stated that he
could not remember but he did add that Janie had
paid cash for part of her purchases and had charged
the rest on that day. It is uncertain from the record
if Williams was unclear about the time or about the
conversation he had with Burchfield.

Gus Blaine testified that he had been deputized and
was sent to get the clothes from the Ed Permenter
home that Swinton had been wearing previously.
He stated that he found the clothes and the two
handkerchiefs in a coat pocket. Under cross-
examination by the prosecution, Blaine said that he
could not remember stating in the first trial that he
had told District Attorney Lamb that he found the
handkerchiefs in a pants pocket.

Hugh Hobby was a young boy, aged thirteen. He
was called as the next witness. His testimony was
that he had been swimming with his two brothers in
Lobutcha Creek not far from the Hinze Post Office.
*(The community of Hinze is located a short
distance from Rural Hill just southeast and across
Lobutcha Creek.)* He indicated that they arrived at
the swimming hole around 2:00 pm and had passed
the mail rider along the way.

When the Hobby boys reached the swimming hole,
they found Swinton Permenter, Lon Burchfield,
Levi Burchfield and Ezra Brazest already there.
(Brazest was probably Brazeal or Breazeale.

Brazeal will be used here as it was most commonly referred to in testimony).

A short time later, they all left the creek together and headed back toward the Hinze Post Office. Hobby testified that along the way, Alonzo Burchfield stated that he had to get back to the field and his plowing. Permenter replied. "It ain't work time yet." Ezra Brazeal pulled his watch out of his pocket and noted that it was 2:25 pm.

Alonzo (Lon) Burchfield who was swimming with Swinton was the next to testify. He indicated that Swinton approached him (while he was plowing) around noon and asked him to go to the swimming hole with him. They stopped at the Hinze Post Office for as much as an hour while Swinton conducted some business there. *(While not indicated here, it had been stated that Permenter was arranging for the purchase and delivery of several bottles of wine.)*

From there, the young men went to the pool and stayed for roughly an hour. Burchfield indicated that they did not pass the mail rider along the way. He also recalled the conversation about the time as they were returning to the Hinze Post Office and that according to Brazeal's watch it was 2:35 pm.

Burchfield then testified that he, Levi Burchfield and Swinton crossed the field he had been plowing and went to the Burchfield house where Levi drew some water for them to drink. He did not know the exact time but in his opinion, it was about 3:20 pm. He then stated that Swinton went with him back toward the field where he was working and they separated at the nearby crossroads. He estimated the time to be 3:30 pm.

Under cross-examination, Burchfield denied hearing Swinton say, "Do you think a man could have plowed all this land from 3:20 till sundown?" *(this referenced the field that Burchfield had been plowing and the statement had been attributed to Permenter by others).*

He also denied making a statement to Walter Cummins that he knew Permenter was guilty and that Permenter had asked him to help move Miss Janie's body to the creek.

Walter Bennett, the mail rider was the next defense witness. Bennett rode the "Star" route from the Vowell Community to Rural Hill. He indicated that the normal schedule was followed that day which included delivery at Rural Hill around noon and leaving that community at around 1:00 pm. He normally arrived at Hinze Post Office at 2:10 pm.

He stated that along the route he did hear a group of young boys shouting and playing at the swimming hole but that it was as much as two hundred yards from the road so he did not see who might have been there. He did meet his uncle and a man named Tom Gregory along the way but they walked ahead as he stopped to water his horse. He looked at his watch as he stopped and noted that it was 2:16 pm. Bennett could not remember passing the Hobby boys along his route.

Several more witnesses were called to confirm the defense's timeline. Medder Hobby, the brother of Hugh, testified that Brazeal's watch indicated 2:35 pm as the group returned to Hinze Post Office. Ezra Brazeal testified that his watch indicated 2:35 pm as well.

The last witness of the day was the mother of Alonzo and Levi Burchfield. Mrs. George Burchfield testified that she had seen Swinton Permenter on the day of Janie's murder for the first time between 12:00 and 1:00 pm. She indicated that her two sons went with Swinton to the swimming hole and that they returned at around 3:30 pm that afternoon.

The defense had been effective in establishing a timeline of Swinton Permenter's activities until roughly 3:30 pm on the day of the murder. If the testimony was believed, it would establish that Swinton had been as much as two miles away from the scene of the murder at or near the time that Janie was last seen around 3:00 to 3:20 pm.

The Saturday session of court adjourned early at 4:00 pm. Testimony would resume on Monday.

CHAPTER 14.
Defense Continues

SUNDAY, AUGUST 18,1912

The court was in recess for the Sabbath. The jury was under the watchful eyes of two bailiffs charged with their care. Jury members were not allowed to attend church but they did have the opportunity to stroll about the small town of Winona for some fresh air and exercise.

A special report in the Commercial Appeal indicated that the defense planned to call witnesses till at least Wednesday. Considering rebuttals and closing arguments, the case would not likely go to the jury before the next Friday.

MONDAY & TUESDAY, AUGUST 18 -19, 1912

Court convened again at 8:30 am as the defense called its next witness, Dillard Vowell. It is believed that Dillard was a nephew of Elbert Vowell who figured so strongly in the case of Ben Walker. The Vowells were relatives of the Permenter family. Dillard confirmed the time frame given by the previous defense witnesses. He related leaving the swimming hole on Lobutcha Creek with the

Burchfields, the Hobbys and Swinton Permenter and noted the time given by Ezra Brazeal as 2:35 pm.

The next witness was George Burchfield, the father of Lon and Levi, the boys who had been with Swinton that day. His testimony supported the timeline given by the previous defense witnesses.

Under cross-examination by Prosecutor Hill, Burchfield denied making a statement to two men, D.R. Dempsey and John Ray that he saw Swinton leave his place at 2:20 not 3:30 as he stated. This statement was supposedly made on the road to Louisville just prior to the first trial.

Burchfield's other son Levi was the next on the stand and he corroborated the other witnesses in reference to the time frame.

The postmaster and owner of the store in the Hinze community was also called to testify. In his statement, he noted that it was about a quarter of a mile from the store/post office to the swimming hole. He remembered that the boys in the group left the post office sometime before the mail rider arrived from Rural Hill. He was not required to keep written records of the arrival and departure of the mail rider so he could not be exact in his timeline but did recall that he saw Lon Burchfield and Swinton Permenter return from the swimming hole.

The parade of witnesses continued throughout the next two days and included several of Permenter's relatives.

Next on the stand was Swinton's sister, Nellie. At the time of the trial, Nellie was twenty-five. She was living in her parents' home at the time of the murder. Nellie stated that on the morning of that day, her father was plowing in a nearby field and by late morning, her mother had left to go to Mr. Schumacher's store in Hinze. She did not want to stay at home alone so around noon she decided to visit her sister who was married to a man named Tom Gregory. The Gregory's lived a short distance away.

She indicated that Swinton left the house shortly before her and was headed to the swimming hole at Lobutcha Creek to meet the Burchfield boys. She stopped at the Burchfield's nearby home before passing the mailbox and going to the Gregory's. She saw her father plowing in the field along the way. Later in the day she saw Swinton returning past the Gregory house toward home.

 She noted the time as 3:45pm as she was concerned that he should have been plowing. She returned home 20- 30 minutes later and saw Swinton plowing in a field across a small branch.

Nellie claimed that she was outside much of the afternoon potting flowers in the yard and observed

Swinton several times throughout the afternoon. At one point, Nellie indicated that Swinton met with his father and exchanged horses and her father left to go to the blacksmith shop to get his plow sharpened.

While the horses were being swapped, she was with Swinton as they ate some apples on the edge of the yard. She could not provide the exact time but noted that it was late afternoon. Swinton then returned to the field and continued plowing till sundown.

Nellie testified that late that afternoon she had spoken with a group of negroes who were living on the Sharp's farm and they informed her that Janie was missing. She indicated that she was the first person to inform Swinton of Janie's disappearance. Her mother had been informed while at the home of Ol' Permenter, Swinton's uncle.

While Nellie was talking to Swinton, the phone rang and their cousin, Lemander Vowell, talked to Swinton and informed him that help was needed in the search. Nellie indicated that Swinton left after supper – just before dark and that she did not see him again until 3:00 am the next morning. Later, Bob McCool and Tom Ray went to the Permenter home and asked for Swinton and if she knew that Janie was missing.

Nellie was then asked about Swinton's clothing. When Swinton left that evening, he was wearing a blue serge coat and a blue checked linen colored shirt. She indicated that when he came home later the next morning, he changed clothes because he had gotten wet during the search. Nellie indicated that she was not at home when the sheriff's officers arrived to get Swinton's clothes.

Nellie was questioned about the handkerchief that was submitted into evidence and had the following to tell the court:

Nellie and many in the community had attended a July 4th picnic at Indian Springs in 1910 prior to the murder. Her now deceased older brother, Walter, found a handkerchief in his buggy while there. He gave the handkerchief to Nellie and told her to tell Swinton to find the owner.

Nellie remembered that a young man named Fletcher Whitney *(possibly Whitmire)* and Janie Sharp had been sitting in Walter's buggy alongside another buggy with Estelle Ray and Bob McCool.

Defense attorney Miller handed Nellie Permenter the handkerchief submitted into evidence and pulled another handkerchief from his pocket and asked her to examine them both. Nellie indicated that there was no difference between them. Miller then submitted both handkerchiefs to the jury for them to examine.

Building on the doubt created by Nellie's testimony about the handkerchief, the defense called J. L. Wilson to the stand. Wilson was at the Sharp home when Janie's body was brought there and placed on a bed. Wilson testified that he saw some bundles, a parasol and a lady's handkerchief either by or on the bed with Janie's body.

Wilson claimed that a young woman named Maggie Morgan was present as well and had remarked that the handkerchief was the one belonging to Janie. When he was cross-examined by the prosecution, Wilson indicated that there were several people in the room at the time and that others had heard Morgan make the comment but he failed to identify anyone else who could validate the statement. He also admitted that at the time of the murder, he was farming land owned by Ed Permenter and that he could not specifically identify the handkerchief.

The defense took a different direction when it recalled Lee Sharp, Janie's brother, to the stand and addressed a series of rumors about the case.

Lee was first questioned about a statement he allegedly made to Henry Ray in a Louisville poolroom. Didn't he say that he would give Ray's wife, a young woman named Effie Permenter Ray and a cousin to Swinton, $100 if she would tell that she saw Swinton kill Janie?

Lee Sharp denied making the offer but did admit that he told Ray that he believed Effie knew about the murder and had seen the act. When he was cross-examined by the prosecution, Sharp indicated that it was actually Ray who first made the statement – "I believe Effie knows all about the murder." Sharp indicated that he then replied, "I do too. I wish she would tell it."

Sharp was then asked if he provided a statement to The Commercial Appeal after the first trial in Louisville about a rumor that Effie Permenter (unmarried at the time of the murder) had witnessed Swinton commit the crime while she was washing near her father's home. Lee provided a vague answer but attributed the rumor to a Mrs. Maddox who lived near Ethel.

Judge McLean intervened at this time and specifically asked Sharp if he had any knowledge of the Detective Ben Walker and Walter Permenter searching for testimony against others that might have committed the crime. He denied any knowledge.

Henry Ray was then called as a witness and he testified that Lee Sharp did make a remark about Effie receiving $100 if she admitted what she knew about Swinton committing the murder.

Effie Permenter Ray was then called to the stand. She was fourteen at the time of the murder and denied ever telling anyone that she saw Swinton commit the crime. She claimed to have seen Swinton that afternoon around dusk.

Swinton's older sister, Mrs. Tom Gregory also claimed to have seen Swinton in the afternoon at 3:45 pm. After some discussion, Judge McLean doubted the accuracy of the time and omitted her testimony from the record.

Ol' Permenter was the next witness called by the defense. Ol' was Swinton's uncle. He was also a mute and his testimony had to be interpreted by a man named J. H. Rose who knew Ol' from his time at a deaf and dumb institute as a young man.

Ol' claimed to have seen Swinton plowing in a nearby field at 4:00 pm and then later again at 4:45 pm as he returned from his brother's home (Ed Permenter) at that time. He testified to the accuracy of the time as he looked at a clock in his home when he stopped for a drink of water.

The last witness on the 20th was a man named Ed Owen. His testimony was immediately suspect and of little consequence. His testimony was limited to a description of tracks in the woods leading away from the location of the body. He stated that he believed the tracks belonged to a man and a woman. It is uncertain as to his testimony in the previous trial, but the newspaper reports indicated that there were some contradictions in his statement. Reports also indicated that in the previous trial, his oath was impeached on the stand.

CHAPTER 15.
Swinton's Testimony

WEDNESDAY, AUGUST 20, 1912

There had been considerable speculation that Swinton Permenter would or would not testify in his own defense. That ended on Wednesday morning as Swinton was the first to take the stand.

Permenter's demeanor was calm, much like it was in the first trial but his soft-spoken manner proved to be a difficulty not only for the spectators but also for the stenographer, the jury and even the attorneys. He was admonished on several occasions throughout his testimony to speak up.

Led by his attorney, he began by describing himself and his relationship with Janie Sharp. He said that he was born near Rural Hill and had known Janie all his life. He acknowledged that he had "kept company" with her as many as five or six times in the past but with other young ladies as well. He said that his interest in those of the opposite sex began at around the age of fifteen. He noted that he had visited Janie's home on half a dozen occasions over the two years prior to her death. The last occasion was on the Sunday prior to her death when he spent the better part of the day there along with a group of other young people after Sunday church service at Rural Hill.

On the day of the murder, July 21, 1910, he spent the morning plowing in a field near his family's home. At around 11:30, he stopped his fieldwork and left for the Hinze Post Office at around noon in the company of the Burchfield boys with the intent of going to the swimming hole after attending to his business at the Post Office.

He gave the Postmaster money to send for four quarts of sherry wine before heading to the swimming hole with the Burchfields. On the way back, he testified that Ezra Breazel had looked at his watch and noted that it was 2:36 pm. He also stated that he stopped along the way to kill a snake and a turtle.

At this point in the newspaper reports, there were some inconsistencies related to the testimony. It is possible that the reporter either misunderstood the testimony or simply made an error. The report indicated that Swinton stated that he also stopped at the store in Rural Hill to pick up a bundle of cloth for his sister who had telephoned the request to the storekeeper. This is highly unlikely. First because the store at Rural Hill would have been as much as three- and one-half miles away, this was not corroborated by any other witnesses and no one saw Permenter in Rural Hill that day prior to the search. It is likely that the store in question was

*located in Hinze and the reporter simply made an
error.*

Swinton claimed to reach the Burchfield home at
3:20, walked toward the field where the older
Burchfield brother was plowing and then separated
from Lon Burchfield at a fork in the road and
headed home.

He stopped by the house and threw the bundle of
cloth through an open window onto a bed before
heading back to the field to continue plowing. He
plowed for roughly an hour and a half until he
stopped to change horses with his father who
needed to carry some plow sweeps to the
blacksmith shop in Hinze to be sharpened.

Swinton then stated that he returned to his
fieldwork and continued plowing till sundown. A
few minutes after he returned home, the telephone
rang and he found out that Janie Sharp was
missing.

Sometime between sunset and dark, Swinton
indicated that he left home and stopped at his
Uncle's home, Ol' Permenter for a period of time
before meeting Tom McCool and Theo Ray on the
road not far from Ol's house. He claimed to have
asked them about the missing girl before heading to
the Sharp place with McCool and Ray. From the
Sharp's they advanced to the Commodore Road and
met a crowd of men involved in the search. Swinton

remained with a group of men as they searched both sides of the Commodore Road until 3:00 am when the search broke up until daylight.

Swinton indicated that he started again at daylight and met other searchers near a field owned by Arthur Ray. Several of the men claimed to find tracks along the way. As part of the search, he walked through the woods when he came upon the crowd that had gathered around Janie's body. He stayed with the crowd as Janie's corpse was taken to the Sharp home. He remained there on the porch of the house for a while and then decided to go home and change because his clothes were wet from the rain during the night. He changed his clothes, put them in a side room, got a pan of water and washed, including his feet before putting on a different pair of shoes.

These shoes became key to his testimony and the evidence. The shoes he claimed to have worn during the search were high-top shoes (meaning above the ankle). The pair he put on that morning were considered low-top shoes. The clothes and shoes he wore before changing were submitted into evidence.

Permenter's testimony and cross-examination now turned to the handkerchief and statements attributed to him by others in previous testimony. His statement related to the handkerchief mirrored that of Nellie Permenter.

Swinton said that his brother, the now deceased Walter, had found the handkerchief while on a picnic with a large group at Indian Springs on the Fourth of July.

Walter indicated that he found it on the ground near his buggy and had asked Swinton to find the owner. Swinton claimed to have put the handkerchief in his coat pocket and simply forgot about it. He had not worn the coat since that time and denied that it had been found in his pants pocket as some had previously stated. He also claimed that he knew nothing about the handkerchief as evidence against him until after his arrest.

His testimony then turned to statements attributed to him. He denied having any ill will toward the Sharp family. He denied making any remarks that could be construed as trying to misdirect the search and he denied any comments about a dog barking at a possum on the night of the search.

His denials continued – he claimed to have never made the statement that the bloodhounds would track him because he had been in the woods near the location of the body and he repeated that he had never said that he had it in for "old man Sharp."

In addition, he denied ever directly saying to Lee Sharp that it might have been a negro that killed Miss Janie. He said other men in the crowd were making suggestions as to who could have committed the crime and he did state that he did not think there was anybody mean enough in the whole county to have killed her. He said that he heard several men say that when she was found, she would likely be bound and gagged and other similar statements.

When asked if he knew of any other young men that had courted Miss Janie. He specifically mentioned Earl Ray and Sol Whitmire. Interestingly, he could not remember if he had ever attended school with Janie.

When asked about the bloodhound, he said that the dog smelled around his father's property and went to the barn lot. Swinton claimed he was on the gallery and when the dog returned to the front of the home, he stepped off the porch and into the yard in an attempt to "test the brute." He said the dog went to a hole of water near the well where he was standing but that the dog never scented him.

Under cross-examination by Prosecutor Hill, Swinton was asked about his brother, Walter who had been killed just the week before. Little was said about this testimony but it was noted that Mrs. Permenter was deeply affected and broke down and wept.

Swinton was then asked about an accusation that had occurred early in the investigation. Hill asked if he had ever been indicted for assault or specifically for assaulting a little girl named Sistrunk.

Permenter quickly denied both allegations but interestingly said that he had never been "convicted" in a justice or circuit court. There was no follow up to this question and no evidence was ever submitted related to these accusations.

While under cross-examination, he stated that – yes, he had been in the company of several young women since receiving the handkerchief from his brother but never thought to find its owner.

Before leaving the stand, Permenter denied previous statements about Janie that were attributed to him. He denied saying to David Steed at a prayer meeting that he would give ten dollars and be willing to spend ten years in jail just to have illicit relations with Miss Janie.

He also denied telling Bob McCool while at the home of Cyrus Ray that Janie was the prettiest girl he ever saw and if he couldn't have her – no one would.

The parade of witnesses for the defense continued throughout the day. W.T. (or W. L.) Horn spoke about tracks that he had seen near an old stump. Out of curiosity, he and several others began their own investigation, searching for tracks and evidence.

They started near Rural Hill and turned onto Commodore Road. Near a small ravine near where the body was found, they found evidence of a struggle and tracks of a woman and a man. There was one man's track near an old pine stump that was clear and well defined. He placed his foot in the track and it matched his shoe almost exactly – his size being an 81/2 or nine. A later comparison of his shoe with the one worn by Permenter that night was made during the trial. They did not match.

Swinton's parents were both called by the defense. Mrs. Permenter stated that as far as she knew her family and the Sharp family had been on friendly terms and she was not aware that Swinton had even had an interest in Miss Janie.

She had left home on the day of the murder at around 2:00 pm. Swinton had already gone to the Hinze Post Office. She went by Ol' Permenter's home where Ol's wife joined her at the home of a neighbor, P. Shumaker They spent the rest of the afternoon there. It was here that she first learned about Miss Janie's disappearance from Earl and Forest Ray.

She returned home near sundown and found Swinton had just returned from the field where he was plowing. When they received the phone call about Miss Janie's disappearance, Swinton left there shortly thereafter without eating supper. He was wearing a blue serge coat and light tan high-top shoes. She did not see him again until the next morning when he came home to change clothes.

At this point, the defense recalled Martha Sharp, Janie's mother. When asked if she had spoken with Mrs. Permenter that evening, she acknowledged that she told Mrs. Permenter that Janie had gone to the store at Rural Hill to get cloth for a waist and she was told to hurry home.

When she did not return, Mrs. Sharp had sent her younger children to find her. This was not noted in her initial testimony. When Janie's body was brought to the Sharp home, she said she could not look at her for a while but had found twenty-five cents of change in a pocket and it appeared that the pocket had been ripped or cut by the murderer.

Tom Gregory, Swinton's brother-in-law took the stand and testified that a week after the murder, he returned to the area and found tracks leading to the location where Janie's body was found. He believed that they were the tracks of a man and a woman.

Swinton's father, Ed Permenter was the next witness. He had not testified in the first trial. He corroborated Swinton's testimony stating that he had been plowing that afternoon, that they had changed horses and that he was sure Swinton had plowed until sundown. He admitted that during the evening of the search, several parties came to the house and inquired about Swinton. He also indicated that he and his family were cooperative and assisted the officers who came to get Swinton's clothes the next morning.

R. P. McAlilly was a justice of the peace in the area at the time and he testified to the state of Miss Janie's body, noting that there was very little blood at the scene.

McAlilly was the last witness of the day as court adjourned until the next morning.

CHAPTER 16.
Final Testimony

THURSDAY, AUGUST 21, 1912

The defense was near the end of its witness list. In fact, the first witness called on Thursday morning was their last.

Alma Ray was a family friend and neighbor. She indicated that she had bought a dozen handkerchiefs for Mrs. Ball previously and Mrs. Ball had distributed them as gifts to her female grandchildren. Janie Sharp was one of those grandchildren.

She admitted that she had not paid much attention to the handkerchiefs and could not remember what kind of border they had. Under cross-examination by the prosecution, she said that while at the Sharp home on the morning after the murder, she had been in the room with Janie's body and had not seen a handkerchief.

The prosecution began its rebuttal by focusing again on the handkerchief. Bessie Ray was called to the stand to identify the handkerchief submitted into evidence. She examined it and was definitive in her identification that it had indeed belonged to Jane. Defense counsel attempted to muddy the waters and question her certainty concerning the handkerchief but she never wavered in her testimony.

George Clark was the next additional witness for the prosecution. As a friend of the family, he made bond for Lon Burchfield who was originally arrested along with Permenter. Just prior to Burchfield's release, Clark was conversing with Burchfield and he told him that it was twenty minutes to two when they left the swimming hole on the day of the murder. This was in direct conflict with the timeline Burchfield testified to earlier in the trial.

Clark indicated that he later visited Burchfield at his home and that they took walks and discussed the case prior to the first trial. In one of these discussions, Burchfield again stated that the time was twenty minutes to two and on another occasion as they were walking near the field he had been plowing on the day of the murder, Clark indicated that it was Burchfield who made the statement, "Do you reckon a man could do this amount of plowing from the time I went to the wash hole and get home at 3:30". This statement had been attributed to Swinton Permenter in earlier testimony.

Clark was asked about the veracity of a previous defense witness. The witness was identified at this juncture as Will Owens but this was most certainly the witness previously identified as Ed Owens. While Owens' testimony was not significant in the defense's case, the prosecution seemed to place importance on his poor character. Clark's testimony was that he did indeed know Owens and found him to be a man of poor character and that his reputation for speaking the truth was lacking.

Tom McCool, Hewlett Ray and Alonzo Hunt were called to speak of the character of Owens. Each had a similar opinion of Owens and Hunt indicated that he knew that Owens had been convicted of assault in Oklahoma Indian Territory at the age of fifteen and had served time in a reformatory in Missouri. Hunt told the court that he would not believe Owens under oath.

Swinton Permenter was recalled by the prosecution and asked about a Sunday before the murder while at a gathering at the Cyrus Ray home. He was asked if Sol Whitney had been keeping time with Miss Janie on that evening and that in his jealousy, did not he say that she was the prettiest girl he ever saw and if he couldn't go with her then nobody else would. Permenter denied making such a statement.

Tom McCool in his testimony indicated that he heard Permenter make that statement.

Hardy Breazel, the father of the Breazel boys who had been at the swimming hole with Permenter was the next to testify and he contradicted his own son's testimony – stating that his son Ezra told him that

the time so often stated by the defense was actually
1:40 pm not 2:25.

J.F Shumacher, the owner of the other store in
Rural Hill was called and testified that Ol'
Permenter had been in his store around 3:50 pm on
the afternoon of the murder and that Miss Janie
had been there earlier in the day. His testimony was
not significant.

The prosecution then presented two additional
witnesses that brought the defense's timeline into
question. Grady Ray stated that she heard
Swinton's sister, Nellie, state on the morning after
the murder while at the Sharp home, that she had
seen Swinton at the Tom Gregory place at around
3:00 pm. Another woman named Iva stated that
she heard Nellie make the same statement.

In rebuttal, the defense did not address this
statement but did call Reese Hobby, who was the
father of the Hobby boys who were at the swimming
hole with Swinton on the day of the murder. Hobby
was called to rebut the testimony of Charlie Horn, a
previous witness for the prosecution. Horn's
testimony was not documented in the Commercial
Appeal's articles but he apparently testified that he
had been with the boys at the swimming hole.
Hobby indicated that Horn did not go to the Hinze
Post Office with his sons but did return with them
after swimming.

Henry Ray was the last witness to testify in the trial.
Henry married Effie Permenter, Swinton's cousin.
He stated that on Christmas in 1911, seventeen
months after the murder, he told his wife if she
knew anything about Swinton's role in the murder
that she had better tell it. She was offered $800 to
tell what she knew *(never stating from where that
money would come)* and that the family had
received a letter stating that she knew all about the
murder and she better tell it or she would get in
trouble.

Both sides rested their case and the court was
adjourned till 9:00 am on Friday morning. Closing
arguments would be made and it was expected that
the jury would receive the case sometime after
noon. After one day of jury selection and nine days
of testimony, the end of the long saga of Janie
Sharp and Swinton Permenter was approaching.

CHAPTER 17.
Final Arguments

FRIDAY & SATURDAY, AUGUST 22-23, 1912

The crowd in the courtroom continued to grow as the press and interested parties wanted to be on hand for the conclusion of one of the most sensational trials in Mississippi history. Not all present were able to fit into the courtroom and the gallery was set aside for women only. The Montgomery County Sheriff brought in more deputies and stationed them about the room fearing that there might be outbursts upon the reading of the verdict. The Commercial Appeal noted that individuals from Starkville, Maben, Indianola and Gulfport were in the crowd.

On Swinton Permenter's side of the room were his parents, sisters Nellie and Eva and his married sisters, Mrs. Gregory and Mrs. Schumaker. Before the session opened, Swinton could be seen playing with one of his nieces at the railing.

On the opposite side were Mr. and Mrs. Sharp, their daughter, Mrs. Morgan and their two remaining sons.

Court opened that morning with controversy. There was much legal haggling over the instructions to the jury. The details under contention were not disclosed but by 10:00 am, the matter had still not been settled and Judge McLean adjourned till 1:00 pm. Over the next few hours, the matter was settled and summations began promptly after lunch.

Judge McLean cautioned the crowd, stating that he would not tolerate any outbursts or expressions of approval or disapproval in his courtroom.

The prosecution began their final argument with Hill as the first to speak. He simply reviewed the case and was considered effective.

He was followed by R. B. Miller for the defense who spoke for nearly two hours, ridiculing the prosecution's case and making a plea for acquittal. J. B. Webb then spoke for the defense pointing out contradictions in the testimony of several of the state's witnesses and closed by stating that the physical facts of the case could point to nothing but acquittal of his client. He possibly suggested other scenarios under which the crime could have been committed.

As darkness began to fall, former Judge J. H. Teat for the prosecution made a passionate case for conviction. His arguments were emotional and appeared to have a deep affect upon the Sharp family.

The case would not go to the jury just yet. There were still arguments to be made that would take a considerable amount of time. At 7:00 pm, Judge McLean told a disappointed courtroom that arguments would resume on Saturday.

****

The next morning, the courtroom swelled with spectators as closing arguments were to continue. As the court convened, Defense Attorney Miller made a motion to close the arguments. His reasoning was that the state had opened and closed the summations on the previous day and both sides had had their opportunities to make their case. Judge McLean was not moved however and he instructed further statements to continue.

Speaking for the defense was W.F. Thompson. Thompson's approach was to castigate the Sharp family and their supporters for their hasty and determined conviction that Swinton Permenter had committed the crime. Their rush to judgment had blinded them to any other possibilities – the real possibility that someone other than Permenter had taken Miss Janie's life on that July day more than two years ago. He appealed to the jury to not allow blind prejudice and passion over the brutal crime to lead to the conviction of an innocent man.

The final statement for the defense was made by H.H. Rogers, one of Swinton's attorneys from the first trial. He reviewed Permenter's alibi in great detail and proceeded to attack any prosecution witnesses that cast doubt upon the timeline. He was especially harsh when it came to Hardy Breazel who contradicted his own son's testimony about the time that the youths left the swimming hole.

Rogers also pointed out that the shoe evidence, initially presented by the prosecution, did not support their case. He noted the testimony by C.B. Ray that indicated that the supposed track of the killer did not match the shoes won by Permenter on the day of the murder.

As it was nearly the noon hour, Judge McLean recessed until 1:00 pm when the prosecution would have its last opportunity to present its argument.

That afternoon, District Attorney Thomas Lamb made the final statement for the prosecution. His approach was to lay out the state's theory of the murder for the jury.

The state contended that Swinton Permenter had not returned to the field to plow that afternoon. That upon returning from the swimming hole at an earlier time than defense witnesses stated, his sister Nellie Permenter had sent him to Rural Hill to purchase some dress goods from one of the stores. Along the route, he met Miss Janie in a lonely spot, forced her into the woods and subsequently killed her in a brutal manner.

He recapped the testimony of numerous witnesses concerning his strange behavior during the search and he also covered the statements attributed to him by others in testimony concerning his desire and interest in Janie. He then cast doubt upon the testimony of Swinton's family members, noting that it would be expected of them to defend him even if it meant lying under oath.

He came to the defense of Hardy Breazel, who had the unenviable task of contradicting his own son on the stand. Lamb indicated that the state believed that the younger Breazel had been threatened with charges of perjury if he did not support the timeline presented by other defense witnesses.

Defense Attorney Miller had presented an alternate theory of the crime in his earlier closing statement. This theory was not documented in the Commercial Appeal article but was now addressed by Lamb.

Miller had apparently suggested that Janie had actually been killed at Rural Hill, her body placed in a sack and carried to the wooded branch by a man and a woman where the body was found. There is no indication as to who these people might have been and was likely one of many rumors that had developed in the community after the crime. Lamb ridiculed the story and said there was no evidence to support it.

Lamb closed his argument with an appeal for the jury to fulfill their responsibility and ensure that justice was done in this case. His final statements were to review the graphic and brutal manner in which Miss Janie Sharp had been murdered.

The emotional arguments were now completed. The Sharp family had endured the process but had wept openly at times. According to newspaper reports, Swinton Permenter seemed calm and showed little emotion during the final statements – just as he had done throughout the trial.

With the final statements made at 3:30 pm, the jury was provided with instruction by Judge McLean and retired to deliberate at 3:55 pm. Permenter remained in the courtroom and was seen smoking a pipe and cigarettes throughout the evening as he waited to learn his fate.

Deliberations continued for four hours without reaching a verdict. At 8:00 pm, the jurors retired for the evening. The trial of Swinton Permenter would continue for at least one more day.

CHAPTER 18.
The Verdict

SUNDAY, AUGUST 24, 1912

This two-year drama began on a county road near
Rural Hill, Mississippi in 1910 with the brutal
murder of an attractive young woman ready to start
her adult life. It was about to culminate in a packed,
sweltering courtroom in the small town of Winona;
a courtroom where the fate of another young person
was to be decided – freedom or death at the end of
a noose.

Through these two years, a whole county was
divided. Feelings ran high and even families were
torn between their support of the victim's family
and the belief in the guilt or innocence of a young
man named Swinton Permenter.

From almost the beginning, the Sharp family never
wavered in their belief in Swinton's guilt. The
Permenter family likewise rallied to their youngest
son, resolute in their certainty of his innocence.
These two years also saw the blatant murders of two
men; murders that were almost certainly tied to the
case- and murders in which no one was ever
brought to justice.

Both sides had presented their cases, evidence was
produced, rebuttals made and lengthy summations

presented. It was now in the hands of a jury of twelve men.

A Sunday court session was a rarity but given the length of the trial and with nothing left to do but wait for the jury to make its decision, Judge McLean stood ready to resume if a verdict was reached. It did not take long.

The jurors began their deliberation early that morning and by 8:50 am, the twelve men of Montgomery County filed back into the jury box. Swinton Permenter stood to hear his fate as his family and the Sharp family looked on in anticipation.

Judge McLean asked, "Gentlemen, have you agreed upon a verdict?'

C.L. Moore, the selected foreman of the jury stated, "Yes, sir, we have."

The slip of paper holding the decision was passed to the Court Clerk named Ford. There was dead silence in the crowded courtroom as all waited for the verdict.

In a deliberate tone, Clerk Ford read,

"We the jury, find the defendant not guilty."

There was no outburst in the courtroom as was feared, no gasp of despair or relief, only a low, almost inaudible murmur. Swinton Permenter seemed stunned; the Sharp family was devastated.

Before dismissing the court, Judge McLean spoke to the jury. He thanked them for their service and stated that the case had been moved to Winona because the court was familiar with the nature of juries in the community and knew that their actions would be just and right.

While he served and respected the people of the whole judicial district, he brought the case to his hometown for those reasons. He again thanked them for their patient consideration of the evidence and the arguments presented by the attorneys and that he believed that the verdict was one based on a fair and impartial consideration of the evidence presented and the law. Their verdict could not be criticized.

The jury foreman C. L. Moore responded and thanked the court and the Montgomery County Sheriff for the many kindnesses extended to them during their confinement and deliberation.

The jury was released and the court dismissed. The Permenter family was elated. While Swinton still sat as if numb, his father, mother and sisters rose and went forward to shake the hands of each juror. Ed Permenter was heard to say, "Thank God, my poor boy is free! He never killed that girl!"

Mrs. Permenter was overcome with emotion as tears flowed down her face. She grabbed her son, kissed him and held him in a long embrace.

In an action that would seem odd or even inappropriate by today's standards, the jury returned to the jury room and were soon joined by the Permenter family. Swinton addressed the jurors – thanking them for their decision.

***

The Sharp family was broken, distraught and angry. While speaking with reporters, Will Sharp bitterly repeated his conviction of Permenter's guilt. ".... a crying shame that such a result could have been reached. If they were to bring another man charged with this crime, I'd say nobody but Swinton Permenter murdered her!"

Lee Sharp, Janie's older brother, was livid. He had been convinced of Swinton's guilt from the beginning and taken an active role in the affair. "He is a scoundrel and it is dangerous to turn loose in any community - such a heartless brute!"

After more than two years of suspicion, months of imprisonment in Louisville, Winona and a Hinds County jail, a conviction, a death sentence and the loss of his brother, Swinton Permenter was now a

free man. Regardless, his life would be changed
forever.

Due to the emotion of the Sharp family and friends,
Swinton was protected by a county deputy
throughout that day until he left Winona in the
evening. His destination was closely guarded; all
that was disclosed – "headed to some point not
known. "

The Sharp's and Permenter's returned to their
homes in Rural Hill that evening by train. Some
evidence suggests that both families took the same
train.

At a stop in the community of Durant, both families
were subjected to curious onlookers, the Sharps
receiving sympathy, the Permenters, the object of
inquisitive stares.

Upon disembarking, the Sharps were met at the
McCool depot by a large crowd who expressed their
sympathy due to the outcome of the case. Lee Sharp
told many in the crowd, "They turned a guilty man
loose."

One of the most sensational trials in Mississippi
history was over, yet there was no resolution to
Janie Sharp's murder; no justice, no punishment,
no sense of closure for her family or for the
communities of Rural Hill, Louisville and Winston
County. The trial may have been over, but the story
was not.

***

KOSCIUSKO COURIER

SEPTEMBER 6, 1912

SOME PRETTY SHARP CRITICISM

The verdict of the jury in the Permenter case is a disgrace to Mississippi manhood. The law that requires a jury where an indictment is for murder to bring in a verdict of guilty as charged, or clear, is a travesty of justice and the courts of Mississippi are a farce.

If it's a case of blind tiger whiskey, or negro crap game, shooting on public highway, carrying concealed weapons where the jury can get the fee and justice the costs, there is no possible doubt of conviction. But let the villain have money to hire lawyers, with the law so fixed that a man who has any sense or can read a paper, or is even qualified to form an opinion, he is disqualified to sit on the jury. None but the most ignorant are jurors and they are made to believe that if there is a shadow of a doubt they shall acquit, and nine tenths of them don't really know what would be a doubt.

Now jurors should be allowed to bring in a verdict of guilty for less than murder in the first degree in such cases, and give verdict for imprisonment for 15 to 15 years.

Now from this Permenter verdict Miss Janie Sharp was not killed or out-raged at all, the whole thing being a nightmare and the jury believes she is still going to the Hinze post office after the mail. That is about all the reasonable doubt the jury could have had, judging from the evidence published in the Commercial Appeal. Now is it any wonder that lynch law is in evidence?

I always try to obey the law, but should a daughter of mine be treated in such a manner, I would kill the villain and any officer who tried to keep me from it, and would join any mob to rid the country of such brutes in this kind of case. If we are to hound the poor devil that sells whiskey or carries a pistol, or the negro who shoots craps to the extreme as is done, and turn rapists and murderers loose on the people, better stop the farce of courts as they now are and let each man protect his own home.

It is almost impossible to convict a scoundrel in Mississippi but an honest and truthful man can't get justice at all for the scoundrel will lie and you are told this makes the "reasonable doubt."

Jehosaphat! how we need some old-fashioned justice meted out from our courts.

The people are holding the laws in contempt and justly so.

Now I suggest to stop all courts until the law can be made adequate for such cases.

Dr. R. J. Heald, M.D.

CHAPTER 19.
Speculation

Whether the public agreed with the verdict or not, observers would agree that the legal system of Mississippi worked as it should in the case of Swinton Permenter. An initial rush to judgment and conviction were overturned on solid grounds and ultimately, a well-structured and ordered trial took place that allowed a jury to weigh all the evidence before passing judgment.

In truth, almost all of the evidence was circumstantial and there was direct conflict of testimony from a multitude of witnesses. An impartial jury had no real option but to find Swinton Permenter not guilty based upon the evidence. But does that mean that he did not commit the crime of murder?

The investigation of the crime left much to be desired. Swinton was arrested and charged quickly and with resources focused on his guilt, there was no investigation into other possibilities. There was little focus on hard evidence or attempts to investigate or exclude others as suspects.

In reality, the investigation of this case was beyond the capabilities of law enforcement. This is not a condemnation of the Winston County Sheriff but simply a reality of the times.

Sheriffs in Mississippi were elected officials and still are to this day. While things have changed considerably and law enforcement has become more professional, at that time, no qualifications were required except to be electable.

Most law enforcement involved breaking up fights, settling disputes between neighbors and rousing the occasional drunkard. There were no real investigative skills, little need for them and certainly no source to obtain them. The concepts of modern-day forensics and chain of evidence were not to be pursued until the latter half of the twentieth century.

Given the lack of a direct eyewitness, possession of a murder weapon or an admission of guilt, the local law probably did the best that they could.

In examining the lack of evidence against Permenter, there are several points that cannot be overlooked:

The murder weapon(s) – It was believed that Janie was struck in the head by a blunt heavy object. Some speculated that it may have been the butt of a pistol. Permenter was seen in the possession of a pistol on the night of the murder but little was made of it. All indications are that it was not examined for blood evidence and no attempt was made to compare it to the wound on Janie's head. Based upon the limited trial records, it was not submitted into evidence. It had been suggested that due to the shape and nature of the wound, the blow was from some type of heavy tool with a square edge and not from the butt of a gun. This may explain why the possible possession of a gun by Swinton was not pursued in the trial.

Janie was stabbed and her throat cut in an apparent attempt to assure her death. A Barlow knife, a relatively small folding pocketknife was found in Permenter's clothes.

Again, it was not examined in detail as it was only casually submitted as evidence as an item in his possession along with the handkerchief. There was nothing to indicate that a search for another knife was ever undertaken.

Blood evidence – The general consensus was that Janie struggled with her attacker and possibly escaped his grasp while he was in pursuit. This, in addition to the brutal nature of the crime, would lead one to believe that there would in fact be blood on the murderer's clothing and person.

The location of the body indicated very little blood was present which suggested that Janie was killed elsewhere and the body placed here after her death. If this was a crime of opportunity as the prosecution suggested, it is likely that Permenter would have also had blood transfer to his clothing in the process of moving Janie's body.

While initial reports indicated that the clothes worn by Permenter on the night of the search were sent to the local college for analysis, no blood evidence was ever submitted during the trial.

Lack of wounds – All evidence indicated that Janie fought her attacker as he pursued her. Knowing that she was fighting for her life and that she was a strong healthy young woman, it would be reasonable to assume that she may have scratched, clawed or bruised the killer. There was no mention of wounds upon Permenter or that he was even examined closely for such wounds.

Walter Permenter's notes did indicate bruises on Swinton but suggested they were the result of horseplay with his friends. The issue was never raised at trial. Either Walter did not disclose this information, law enforcement did not examine his person or the prosecution found the information to be inconsequential.

The body and the crime scene – Janie's body and the crime scene were not examined properly. Given the emotion at the time, this could be expected. Considering the despair of the family, the sensibilities of the time, the condition of the body and the heat of a July summer, Janie was buried quickly leaving some questions forever unanswered.

The crime scene was likely a mess. With a crowd of searchers and later curious "investigators," any evidence would have been trampled or contaminated. Tracks attributed to the killer could have just as easily been those of any in the crowd.

Opportunity – The swimming hole on Lobutcha Creek was three and one half to four miles from Rural Hill, no short distance on foot or even by horseback. The Permenter home was four miles from Rural Hill as stated in the trial. Under the defense scenario, it would have been nearly impossible for Swinton to have returned to the Hinze post office and then after leaving the Burchfields make his way to the Commodore Road near Rural Hill and commit the crime at the time estimated. It would then also indicate that his sisters and father had lied on his behalf under oath.

If the defense's timeline was incorrect, it would require that the Burchfield boys, and the Hobbys were either all mistaken about the time or they were all lying for Swinton. And again, it would require his sisters and father to participate in the lie.

Motive – Much was made of previous comments by Swinton concerning Janie, comments that seemed inappropriate in hindsight. Unfortunately, such comments are commonly made by young men about young women and are not necessarily grounds for a murder conviction.

Was there more to the relationship between Swinton and Janie Sharp than was exposed in the trials? Probably. Will Sharp's almost immediate suspicion that Janie may have eloped with someone other than her proclaimed fiancée, Earl Ray and his request for Doctor Clemmons to search for Permenter on the afternoon of the murder suggests that he suspected some sort of relationship between the two young people.

The immediate suspicion cast upon Swinton, particularly by Janie's brother, Lee, also indicated that he believed that there was more to the relationship. Speculation on this relationship has run rampant over the years and some have suggested that Janie's engagement to Earl Ray was a ruse perpetrated to hide her love affair with Swinton from a disapproving father.

The handkerchief was the strongest evidence presented by the prosecution in both trials. It was the one piece of physical evidence that could tie Swinton to the crime.

But there were problems here that the jury could not likely overlook. Swinton had a plausible explanation for its possession that was supported by his sister's testimony – a found item, forgotten and tucked into a coat pocket. When taken with the uncertainty of whether the handkerchief was found in Swinton's coat pocket or his pants pocket and that one witness testified that she saw a handkerchief near the body as it lay in the Sharp home, the evidence was not conclusive.

If the handkerchief was found in a coat pocket, a coat that may not have been used on a regular basis, it is feasible that it had been there for some time (*since the July 4th picnic*). If found in a pants pocket, it would be more difficult to explain.

The bloodhound's identification yields some interesting possibilities but again, any conclusion becomes clouded. Did Ruth Hindoo scent Swinton that morning in the yard of the Permenter home as his trainer and several witnesses testified or was the dog's behavior more indecisive than stated? Were the hound's actions influenced by his trainer and the crowd?

The other possibility remains that because Swinton had been in those woods earlier, the dog tracked him rather than the real killer. Even more intriguing, is the possibility that the killer or killers were in the crowd with Swinton outside the Permenter home.

Much was made of Swinton's behavior on the night of the search. Several, including Lee Sharp testified that Swinton at times acted disinterested, evasive and made misleading statements in a possible attempt to lead the searchers away from the body. On the stand, Permenter denied making these statements. He either lied to protect himself or a number of others lied in an attempt to wrongfully incriminate him. This certainly presented a dilemma for the jury.

***

Despite all these issues, there are some circumstances under which Swinton could have committed the crime. Three possibilities seem to stand out:

If the prosecution's timeline was correct and Swinton returned home a full forty-five minutes earlier that the defense presented and if his family was lying to cover his involvement, there would be sufficient time for him to have traveled the distance, especially on horseback. If he had traveled to Rural Hill on an errand for his sister, it is highly likely that he could have encountered Janie on Commodore Road and committed the bloody act. However, this would have required the Burchfields and the Hobby's to provide misleading testimony concerning the time.

This raises another possibility that someone else who had been at that swimming hole could have participated in the murder, helped Swinton cover his tracks and concocted a different timeline to hide their involvement.

The third possibility is intriguing but less likely. If Swinton and Janie were lovers, had they arranged a clandestine meeting on that afternoon? Had Janie rejected his advances or had she informed him of her plans to marry Earl Ray? Had this rejection resulted in a fit of rage leading to Swinton making good on the statement attributed to him - "If he couldn't go with her, nobody else would?"

The fact that there was little effort to investigate any other possibilities concerning the murder is disturbing. It does seem unlikely that an outsider could have committed the crime. No one saw any strangers in the area and they would have been noticed in such a small and close-knit community but there were others from the community who could have committed the act.

It was a rural area and it could certainly be a crime of opportunity – a young woman walking alone would seem an easy target.

Swinton had made the statement in prison that he believed he knew who committed the crime and that they had testified against him (at least in the first trial) His implication was that there were two men involved although it was never stated publicly who he believed they were.

Thomas McElroy and Hewlett Ray were the most likely candidates due to their "arrest" by Ben Walker. But no evidence was ever presented to show their involvement and the complete and utter dismissal of any evidence by the prosecution would suggest that they had no involvement. It appears that it will always remain a mystery as to the identity of the four witnesses who failed to appear at McElroy's and Ray's hearing.

In closing arguments, the possibility that Janie had actually been killed while in Rural Hill and that a man and woman had been involved (almost certainly local folk) seems farfetched as well. No evidence was ever provided to support this theory or to identify the parties involved.

It is interesting to note that no suspicion was cast upon any blacks in the community. Given the nature of the times, it is certain that if there had been any evidence in that direction, it would have been investigated further. Nothing in statements or trial testimony cast any suspicions in that direction.

Over the years, various theories have been put forward concerning who killed Miss Janie Sharp and almost all without substance and certainly without evidence.

CHAPTER 20.
Effie

Effie Brown Permenter was a young girl, only fourteen at the time of the murder of Janie. Over the years, her role or lack thereof in the case has led to much rumor and speculation.

Effie was a cousin of Swinton's and the daughter of Ol' Permenter. Between the time of the murder and the second trial, she married Henry Ray, who was a cousin of Earl and Hewlett and a nephew of Cyrus Ray. This marriage was certainly a complication for her due to their support of the Sharps and presented a trying situation resulting in torn loyalties.

Almost from the beginning, strong rumors circulated through the communities of Rural Hill and Hinze that Effie had seen something sinister on the afternoon of the murder of Janie. The proximity of the Ol Permenter home certainly made this a possibility. Ol's house was the closest to the murder scene where Janie's body was found, on a ridge approximately only a quarter of a mile away, located to the east and slightly south of the crime scene.

It was obvious from her questioning during the second trial that some strongly believed that Effie knew more than she was willing to disclose - that she saw the crime or at the very least heard screams on that afternoon. On the witness stand, Effie denied any knowledge of the crime and supported the defense's timeline.

Lee Sharp believed that Effie knew more than she admitted. He obviously believed or even perpetuated the rumor that Effie had seen Swinton commit the act. Lee's belief was referenced in the trial testimony although he attributed the source of the rumor to another individual. It is likely that he offered money through her husband– in one case $100 and possibly as much as $800 for her to tell what she knew. Her husband, Henry Ray testified that the family had received a letter stating that she knew all about the murder and she better tell it or she would get in trouble. The source of that letter is unknown.

Publicly, Effie vehemently denied any knowledge of the crime yet the rumors persisted. Most of the local talk indicated that Effie was in the yard of her home washing clothes at the time of the murder. Upon hearing screams, Effie ventured closer and saw the murder and the murderer(s). The Sharps were so certain of Swinton Permenter's guilt that they did not doubt or question that Effie had most certainly seen Swinton commit the act on that afternoon.

Others were not so sure. Many believed that she saw the murder but the culprit was not Swinton

Permenter and that she was the subject of
intimidation – too afraid to speak out.

Many years later, a statement surfaced, the veracity
of which cannot be proven. A handwritten note
between family members referenced secondhand
knowledge of statements made by Effie many years
after the murder and trials. This statement was not
dated, cannot be verified as to the source and was
certainly not written by Effie.

The note indicates that Effie relayed the following
story to a family member:

On the afternoon of the crime, Effie heard Janie's
screams and ran toward the crime scene. From
hiding, she saw two men, neither of which was
Swinton Permenter, commit the act.

Frightened, she remained in hiding until the men
left the scene. In shock and still hidden, Effie saw
the men return and cut Janie's throat to ensure her
death. Effie identified the men who were well
known in the community.

A second attached note referenced a deathbed
confession to family members, made by a man in
his old age. It indicated that he also made a
confession to a local attorney.

Historical information indicates that one of the men
in question did not live to old age.

The second note did not specifically name the man but clues provided in the document could reference either man.

One is left to question the story as a whole or part. Did Effie tell someone that she saw the murder but was then too intimidated to acknowledge what she saw *(which is suggested by the note writer)* or was this just a case of rumor at the time of the murder perpetuated over the years to enhance the tale? If she did see the act, it would seem unlikely that she would not testify to help a family member.

Given the lack of any hard evidence, the secondhand nature of the statement and Effie's testimony in the second trial, it would be irresponsible to reveal the identity of the men referenced in the document.

I will acknowledge that the men in question were local residents, well known and that they provided testimony that was generally detrimental to Swinton in the trials.

It is interesting to note that this information also closely corresponds with a statement made by Swinton Permenter to one of his jailers while incarcerated at the Hinds County Jail after the first trial:

"He has discussed the murder of Janie Sharp with me some, as he has with everyone who visits him, but has never said anything that could be

construed into even an intimation that he committed the crime. He has, on the contrary said he believed two other fellows committed the crime and these two men from what I understand were active in the prosecution.... He seems to think everything will turn out right in the end and I believe it will."

Did Swinton's belief that two others committed the crime stem from Effie, the work of the detective Ben Walker or was it just an attempt by Swinton to "muddy the waters" and cast doubt upon his own guilt?

To my knowledge, no solid evidence exists to corroborate Effie's witnessing of the crime. There are however several other references that do indicate that others, possibly two individuals, may have been involved in the crime and also hearsay that there was in fact, a death bed confession.

Effie had four children with Henry Ray. After his death in 1934, she married Sam Moss. She died in Memphis in 1950 and is buried in the Parkway Cemetery in Kosciusko in Attala County.

CHAPTER 21.
Louis

Over the years, interest in the case would peak from time to time. In the 1950's, 60's and early 70's when talk began to gravitate toward the mystery of her death and who the guilty party might be, unverifiable accounts of anonymous phone calls and threats would attach themselves to the tale. With no new evidence or a confession, the talk eventually slowed.

In the 1980's and 1990's, a local man named Louis Taunton sparked interest in the case again. Taunton was an amateur genealogist, schoolteacher and one-time Mayor of Louisville who had compiled a number of books on Winston County history; reprinting newspaper articles and working with others to compile a cemetery index. Through much of this time, he also provided a weekly newspaper column of "yesterday's news."

Taunton certainly had an interest in the case and had on several occasions spoken about the murder before organized groups in the area. He did his part in perpetuating the mystery of the case and maintaining interest.

Taunton told similar but not necessarily the "same" story to different groups and individuals – sometimes intimating that he knew the identity of the killer(s), sometimes indicating that he had proof, sometimes not.

Depending on the source, some believed that he was in the process of writing a book about the Janie Sharp case prior to his death while others were convinced (based upon their conversations with Taunton) that the book had been completed. The status of that book is just another offshoot of the mystery of the Janie Sharp case.

Taunton had told some individuals that the manuscript for the book was complete. In the manuscript, he supposedly named the killer – a killer who confessed on his deathbed to a local attorney. Taunton indicated to others that the attorney maintained a client/attorney confidence for many years before disclosing the information.

Taunton then indicated that he held the publication of any book until a final family member of the confessor had passed away. It is at this point that the account of the book begins to twist and turn like a leaf in a Pearl River whirlpool.

According to some, upon the death of that family member, Taunton took the manuscript to a literary attorney for review prior to publication. By accounts, the attorney discouraged the publication of the book due to concerns of libel. Taunton weighed his options and according to some, he abandoned any plans to publish his work and the manuscript never saw the light of day.

When one reviews the whole tale of the Taunton book, a number of questions and inconsistencies arise that only deepen the mystery:

Did the manuscript actually exist? There are those who are certain that it did but I have been unable to find anyone that can provide reasonable firsthand knowledge. If it did exist – what happened to it?

- It is possible that Taunton destroyed it but as a writer myself, that seems unlikely given the amount of work and research required for such an undertaking. It is one thing to choose to not publish a work but it is something entirely different to destroy it. If it existed and if it was not destroyed, it has not surfaced in the years after Taunton's death.

- Given the historical nature of such a manuscript and the level of research involved, it is likely that the only libelous aspect of such a book would be if the author made a direct accusation without documentable proof. If there were proof beyond hearsay, there would be no risk of libel and without proof, it would be irresponsible to make such an accusation. There was nothing in Louis Taunton's character that would leave one to believe him to be irresponsible or reckless in such matters. It would also seem that given the amount of work and time involved in producing such a work, it would be realistic to expect an author to simply rewrite those sections of the book that might be questionable. While it may dampen the dramatic aspect of the work, it would still be of interest and have important historical significance.

- According to some, a local attorney heard the confession of the guilty party on their deathbed and only many years later disclosed the details to Taunton. This would likely be Taunton's source as to the identity of the killer. One would have to question why this attorney would choose to break his silence and why he would choose Taunton as his confidant.

- Taunton disclosed to at least one individual that the murderer of Janie Sharp was married at the time of her death and had two young children. This may have been a way for Taunton to provide clues without naming the party involved. In an interesting twist, one of the individuals named as the killers in the Effie Permenter document fit that description perfectly.

Information related to Louis Taunton's research and possible manuscript may yet surface. The full truth will likely never be told. In 2006, Taunton passed away suddenly of a heart attack.

It has been reported that Taunton's wife, Joan, had planned to donate his papers (including any related to this case) to the Winston County Library but Mrs. Taunton has since passed away as well and most of his papers never materialized. Some have reported that the hard drive of the computer believed to hold the book draft was found to be

erased clean - just another mystery in the case of
Janie Sharp.

CHAPTER 22.
The Aftermath

The saga of Janie Sharp began on a lazy summer day in 1910. Because of the unsolved nature of the murder and the related crimes that followed, in many respects, it continues today. The two-year ordeal included a trial and conviction, a Supreme Court ruling that overturned the conviction, suspicions and accusations cast upon others, the murders of two men and a second trial that was a sensation across Mississippi and the South.

Rumors and bad blood would fester like an open wound for most of the twentieth century across a once close-knit community.

When the Mississippi dust settled, no one was brought to justice for Janie's murder or those of Ben Walker, an investigator of the crime, or Walter Permenter, the brother of the suspect. To this day, no one can say who committed these crimes and anyone who may have had firsthand knowledge of the events of the day are long gone.

The Sharp's were convinced of Swinton's guilt and made no further attempts to find any other suspects. In spite of the trial result, they were convinced of Swinton Permenter's guilt and never entertained the thought that some other party might be responsible.

There is no evidence that local law enforcement made any further investigation – not into Janie's murder or those of Ben Walker and Walter Permenter. Either the authorities believed that Swinton Permenter got away with the murder of Janie Sharp or there was simply no further evidence or more likely, there was no desire to pursue the case further. According to some reports, the costs associated with the trials nearly bankrupted the county.

The lack of closure in the case fueled debate, hard feelings and suspicion not only in Rural Hill but in much of Winston County. Almost everyone was a relation or a friend to one or both families. Speculations and accusations continued for many years after the crime and in some forms still exist today.

The people of Rural Hill and Winston County went back to their farms and businesses and continued their lives. Louisville continued to grow and became a center of the timber and heavy equipment industry, a quiet and mostly peaceful little community in central Mississippi.

But what happened to the principal characters in this story?

Cyrus Ray (Janie's Uncle) and his family stayed in the Rural Hill area and many of the family are buried in the Rural Hill church cemetery.

Walter Permenter was killed by a shotgun blast in 1912 in Eupora. His murder was never solved. No record of his murder or its investigation can be found in county records. The only references to his death can be found in newspaper reports. He is buried at the Masonic Cemetery in the center of Louisville, Ms.

He left a pregnant widow (Madie or Maudie) and two children. She soon left Rural Hill and moved to Kemper county and then Philadelphia, Ms. where she raised her children. She never remarried. She died in 1969 and is buried next to her husband in Louisville.

Hewlett or Hulett Ray, one of the two men accused by Ben Walker of the crime moved to Oklahoma sometime before WW1 where he registered for the draft. He and his wife raised five children and he lived to a ripe old age in Oklahoma and is buried there.

Thomas McElroy (also accused by Ben Walker) was married to a sister of Hewlett and Earl Ray. Little is known about his whereabouts after his dismissed grand jury hearing and most assumed he returned to Texas. It is possible that he stayed in the area but it is certain that he returned at some point. He and his wife are buried at Doty Springs Cemetery in Attala County not far from Rural Hill. He passed away in 1946 at the age of seventy-three.

Doctor William M. Clement and his family eventually left the Rural Hill community and moved his practice to Louisville. He died in 1939 and is buried in the Masonic Cemetery.

While Forrest Ray did not appear to play a significant role in the Janie Sharp case, his tragic death on Christmas Day in 1920 did stir interest. After the trial, he moved his family to the Beaumont- Port Arthur, Texas area where he served as a policeman in the community of Sour Lake.

In the early morning hours of Saturday, Christmas Day, Ray was on duty and sitting in the unfinished vestibule of a new office building under construction. A young man approached on the street and fired five shotgun blasts through a plate glass window striking Ray several times. Ray initially survived the attack but passed a few hours later. A young oilfield worker named Sidney Oliver was taken into custody, tried and convicted of the crime. The motive for the crime was never clear. Strangely enough, after multiple trials, Oliver was ultimately sentenced to five years in prison but served only one year for the act.

Ben Walker was killed in 1912 in the home of Elbert Vowell in Winston County. His killer was never captured or identified. There is no record of further investigation into his death beyond the night he died. Nothing is known about his past and his body was never claimed by family members. Some have suggested that he came from the Mississippi Delta but research has been futile. It is highly likely that he used a false name and we may never know his true identity. He is buried in the Smallwood or Wood Cemetery located a few miles south and west of Rural Hill.

Earl Ray, the "fiancé" of Janie Sharp, married in 1914 and continued to live in Mississippi and the general area. He raised several children and passed away in Choctaw County in the 1960's.

Elbert Vowell is believed to have remained in the area but is sometimes referenced as James Elbert Vowell. There is some evidence that he moved to Leake County, Mississippi by 1930.

W.J. Tabor, the employer of Walter Permenter and possible financial contributor to Swinton's defense was a prominent businessman in Louisville. His support of the Permenters generated bad feelings with some in the Rural Hill area.

On January 8, 1913, his home *(known as the "old Liebenfield House)* on East Main Street was destroyed by fire. There was no evidence of foul play. In April 1913, fire destroyed most of a city block in downtown Louisville, including a livery and six structures including a bank, the post office, several other offices and the store of W.J Tabor. The fire was the subject of a variety of rumors including accusations against Tabor. In the following week's paper, Tabor issued this statement: *"It has been intimated or rumored that I fired or had fired the stable that caused the April 21 fire in Louisville. Any man or men who intimated such is a willful, malicious liar and is destitute of principle as a man can be. W. J. Tabor"*

Judge George A. McLean's term as Circuit Court Judge expired in September, 1912. The conduct of the final trial of Swinton Permenter was a sort of triumph for him after the earlier conviction was overturned. Almost immediately after the trial, he was honored by the local bar for his service on the court.

The Will Sharp family stayed in Rural Hill for a short while after the trial, but in 1913, they sold their property and most of the immediate family packed their belongings and moved to Bryan, Oklahoma. Much of the family still live in that area today.

Janie's Father, Will, passed away in 1919 at the age of sixty-one. Martha Sharp suffered a stroke not long after the trial and lived her remaining years as an invalid. She passed just one year after her husband in 1920. They are buried in Calera, Oklahoma. Lee Sharp lived until the age of sixty-nine and is buried in Texas.

At the time of the move, the Sharp's property in Rural Hill, including the house, was sold to Jesse Barfield. The home burned to the ground in 1921.

The Permenter family stayed in Mississippi although at some point, they sold their property in Rural Hill. Records show that Swinton's parents, Edward and Anna are buried in the Hopewell Baptist Cemetery in Choctaw County, Mississippi.

Edward died in 1932 and Anna passed away in 1942. Swinton's brothers and sisters stayed in Mississippi as well and at least one stayed in the immediate area.

Swinton Permenter's whereabouts immediately after the trial are not known. It is doubtful that he ever returned to the Rural Hill area for any length of time.

Much of the following information here is not verifiable but was accumulated from various sources. It is believed that he lived for a period of time in Okolona, Mississippi in the home of his sister.

He entered military service during WW1. Some records indicated that he initially enlisted under the false name, Jesse Jackson. If so, this was corrected as later military records include his real name. These records indicate that he was born in 1895. This was incorrect as he was seventeen at the time of the murder.

There is also evidence that he lived and worked in the oil fields in Texas and Oklahoma but he is listed in the 1930 census as a resident of Bolivar, County,

Ms. and residing in the household of his younger sister.

At some time after 1930, he married a woman named Bernice from Avery County, North Carolina and it is believed that he lived in that area for a period of time. There is little information about the marriage and no indication of children.

In his later years, Swinton suffered from health problems and suffered paralysis in his legs and possibly his hands. As a result, he spent the last years of his life in a Veterans' Administration home in Johnson City, Tennessee as this was listed as his last address.

Swinton Permenter died on August 16, 1946 and is buried at the Mountain Home National Cemetery in Johnson City, Tennessee. There is no evidence that he spoke of the trial in later life and it is probable that those around him knew nothing about the murder of which he was accused.

Janie Sharp lost her life on July 21, 1910. She is buried not at Rural Hill but in the Center Ridge Methodist Church Cemetery located several miles east of Rural Hill. This cemetery was probably chosen because her sister, an infant, was previously buried here.

***

The following photograph was provided by a grand nephew of Janie Sharp. While uncertain as to the purpose of the photograph, it was likely taken in early 1910 and includes many of those involved in the case.

Row 1 – Dallas Wesley Morgan, Gus Whitmire, Hewlett Ray, Thomas McElroy, Clark Hunt. Row 2 – Mae Sharp, Bessie Sharp, Eula Shumaker, Janie Sharp, Estelle Ray

****

Janie Sharp's murder was never solved. It has now been more than one hundred years since her brutalized body was found just off Commodore Road in the Rural Hill Community. It has almost been that long since the unsolved murders of Ben Walker and Walter Permenter. Over that time the area has changed significantly.

Rural Hill was never more than a small village but it was full of life. Two stores, a post office, a church, a two-room school and even a small mill that produced wooden spokes were the center of a small group of farms and the families that worked them.

There was no railroad and no county courthouse and it was inevitable that Rural Hill would slowly decline like hundreds of other communities across Mississippi and the South. Over the years, the Post Office closed and mail delivery moved to McCool. The school was consolidated and closed. Automobiles became more affordable and travel became quicker and easier and the need for the stores diminished as well.

Today, there is no evidence of any structures except for the church. Rural Hill United Methodist Church suffers from declining membership and no longer holds regular services but it continues to survive and is well maintained. Memorial in May always draws a crowd of people whose ancestors founded the Church or grew up within its shadow.

The Commodore Road along which Janie's body

was found, was never much more than a trail. Its location is now on private property and is no longer maintained.

The Neal Ray Road where the Sharp home and the Permenter home were located does still exist and although it is a very narrow, gravel thoroughfare, it is well maintained by the county. The homesteads are long gone but one can identify the locations that might indicate the old homesites.

There are still a few folks who believe they can specifically identify the location where Janie's body was found. In my conversations, I find that there is little agreement as to that location. Using the trial map, reviewing testimony and Walter Permenter's notes, I believe that the location can be identified within a few yards. It is located on private property and not accessible to the public.

I was contacted by an individual who provided helpful information that indicated that some evidence of Janie's moss-covered tracks (heel prints) may have existed into the 1960's although I find this very unlikely.

Janie Sharp's grave is located in the Center Ridge United Methodist Church Cemetery. It is the tallest monument in the cemetery and located near the road. A sister who died as an infant is buried beside her.

Her epitaph reads as follows:

"Sleep On, Dear Janie, Thy Work is Done

Thy Mortal Pangs are O'er

Jesus Has Come And Borne Thee Home

Beyond This World Of Sin And Woe"

At one time, the monument was vandalized and the top marble ornament was removed. It was found along a roadside. Since that time, gracious church members provided the means to restore the monument and attach the top ornament permanently. It has become a favorite place for teenagers to gather at Halloween and the area is the subject of many ghost stories that of course, involve Janie and her murder.

EPILOGUE
A Century of Rumors

*There are a great deal of details and mostly
hearsay about this event that were not initially
included in the original book; some because they
were merely rumor, others because they may not
have been pertinent as told. I include some of them
here – not to lend them credence or to dismiss
them but only as a matter of curiosity:*

One interesting bit of information not previously
included was a Winston County Journal article that
indicated that a local man, Gus Burns found a set of
bloody clothes in a paper sack hidden under a fallen
log, almost immediately after the final trial in 1912.
It stated that the garments consisted of
undergarments and socks and showed much decay
but may have had blood on them. The article stated
that the garments were to be brought to the sheriff's
office for examination. After that article, no further
mention of these garments was ever made. It is not
known by this writer if they ever existed, or were
never submitted to the sheriff, or determined to not
be pertinent to the case. In any event, they were
never mentioned again.

***

There were reports that shortly after the final trial,
the circuit clerk of Winston County received an

anonymous letter postmarked in Memphis, Tennessee. According to the story, the writer confessed to the murder and claimed to be a stranger traveling through the community. Upon finding Janie alone in a lonely place, he murdered and raped her before leaving the area unseen. No such letter has ever surfaced nor can the story be confirmed.

***

According to a family member, Elbert Vowell left the Rural Hill area soon after the final trial in 1913. It is uncertain if this was before or after the family home burned to the ground. Family lore indicates that the Vowell family and Walter Bennett, *(the mailman who testified in the trial)* received numerous threats over the years.

***

Swinton's youngest sister, Laura Ellen, met her future husband, Grover Cleveland Ingram, at the final trial in Winona.

***

There were at least two sources that indicated that there was a romantic relationship between Janie Sharp and Swinton Permenter and that they were seeing each other without her parents' knowledge or consent. Some have indicated that several young women of Janie's age had acknowledged that Janie and Swinton Permenter were romantically involved and that the relationship with Earl Ray was a cover to hide this relationship from her father who disapproved of Swinton.

Another report indicates that Earl Ray had affection for Janie and kept a photograph of her in his possession till his death. This would seem to contradict his participation in such a ruse.

***

A memorial fund was established to pay for Janie Sharp's monument in the Center Ridge Cemetery. Donations ranged from $0.10 to $2.50 by individuals. The list of donors was published in the Winston County Journal.

***

Some believe that the murder of Ben Walker was committed as a "murder for hire" and speculate that a man in the area known as a "dangerous individual" had committed the act for a small sum of money.

***

There were several reports, particularly in newspapers in other parts of the country, that the lynching of Swinton at the time of his arrest and before the first trial in Louisville was a real possibility. One paper indicated that a group of men armed with Winchester rifles had surrounded the town of Louisville and were waiting to ambush the Sheriff and his twenty deputies who were returning Permenter from Montgomery County for trial. This paper also stated that the Governor of Mississippi had called troops to the scene to keep order.

Other papers referenced a mob of a thousand waiting at the railroad station in Louisville upon Swinton's arrival and that the sheriff and his men had difficulty making their way through the crowd to the county courthouse. It also indicated that some had declared that Swinton "must die whether or not the jury convicted him."

These reports were at best – an exaggeration and possibly completely false.

***

A persistent rumor of a deathbed confession by an elderly man related to the case continues to surface but no evidence of such a confession has ever been presented.

***

All those with firsthand information in this case have passed long ago. Without the discovery of some long-lost document or signed confession, the tragic death of Miss Janie Sharp will forever remain a mystery and a subject of debate.

The tragic tale of Janie Sharp has remained a topic of discussion in the area for more than one hundred years. Speculation, hearsay and the examination of the evidence has become a favorite pastime amongst the people of the area. Conversations passed from generation to generation with undoubted elaboration, continue to fuel debate. There are some who believe they know the identity of the killer(s) but without solid evidence, any reference here would be inappropriate.

Most, however, admit that the case is baffling and will forever remain unsolved.

I would be amiss if I didn't give credit to two compilations about the Janie Sharp event. THE TRIAL for the MURDER of PERNINAH JANIE SHARP by Lucille Wood and TRIAL OF SWINTON PERMENTER FOR THE MURDER OF MISS JANIE SHARP JULY 21,1910 by Ruby C. Hurt. Both of these books are available at the Winston County Library and I encourage those who are interested to take a closer look at these compilations of news reports and trial transcripts. They contain more details and contradictory information.

SOURCES

- THE TRIAL for the MURDER of PERNINAH JANIE SHARP by Lucille Wood
- TRIAL OF SWINTON PERMENTER FOR THE MURDER OF MISS JANIE SHARP JULY 21,1910 by Ruby C. Hurt.
- Winston County Journal – Louisville, Ms.
- The Commercial Appeal – Memphis, Tn.
- The Jackson Daily News – Jackson, Ms.
- The Columbus Commercial
- Winston County Circuit Clerk
- Winston County Library – Louisville, Ms.
- Attala County Library – Kosciusko, Ms.
- Tupelo Man – the Life and Times of George McLean, a Most Peculiar Newspaper Publisher by Robert Blade
- http://www.genealogy.com
- http://www.msrailroads.com
- http://msgw.org
- Star Herald – Kosciusko, Ms.
- Star-Ledger – Kosciusko, Ms.
- Kosciusko Star – Kosciusko, Ms.
- Kosciusko Courier – Kosciusko, Ms.
- A History of Winston County, Volume 2, by Jennie Newsom Hoffman
- The Progress Warden – Eupora, Ms.
- Beaumont Enterprise – Beaumont, Tx.
- The Palestine Journal – Palestine, Texas
- http://www.findagrave.com

- http://www.ancestry.com
- Interview with Harry Bernard Tabor –
  Winston County, Ms.
- Winston County, Ms. Sheriff Jason Pugh
- http://winston.msgen.info
- Linda Belongia Neuman
- Murray Black
- Penny Sharp

Other Works by W. W. McCully

Murder in Rural Hill – 2016

Bones of Mississippi - 2022

Made in United States
Cleveland, OH
18 December 2024

12181064R00138